R/c

Books should be returned or renewed by the last date above. Renew by phone **03000 41 31 31** or online *www.kent.gov.uk/libs*

Straightforward Guides

© Doreen Jarrett 2015

ISBN 9781847165251

Printed by 4Edge Ltd www.4Edge.co.uk

Cover design by Bookworks Islington

Contents

Introduction

****

Introduction

This is the first edition of A Straightforward Guide to The Rights of Disabled people. The book is aimed primarily at people with physical disabilities and is wide ranging, dealing with everything from benefits, employment travel, rights in the home and disabled servicemen and women.

Currently, at the time of writing, 2015, there are real fears that the benefits and security enjoyed by people with disabilities are under attack, mainly through the governments approach to reducing the overall welfare bill. It is feared that the introduction of benefits such as Personal Independence Payments, which replace Disability Living Allowance for those under 65 and also the abolition of the Independent Living Fund, will in the longer-term have an effect on disabled people and their incomes. This is because, in the main, disabled people find it harder to enter the workplace and sustain employment that others.

This book covers the benefit system in it's entirety and highlights what you may or may not be entitled to. It also covers carer's rights and the new law governing those rights, the Care Act 2014. Form thereon we discuss employment law as it affects disabled people, education, care homes, rights whilst in hospital,, rights in the home, disabled children,, rights whilst travelling, rights for ex-service personnel and general rights covering the payment of income tax.

Finally, at the end of the book there are useful addresses and websites of organisations who deal with all areas of disability.

This book sets out to educate and inform those with physical disabilities, their carer's and also parents of disabled people, whether adult or child.

Chapter 1

The Law and Disability

The law and disability

In general, the wide body of laws that protect all people in the United Kingdom will apply to disabled people. Such laws can include consumer law, employment law and family law. However, in certain important respects, the law that applies to disabled people, and gives an extra layer of protection is the Equality Act 2010. This law is wide ranging and incorporated many previous Acts, such as the Disability Discrimination Act, and also clearly defines discrimination. Below is a summary of the Act. However, as we go through the book continuous reference will be made to the Act as it applies to the many areas of life, such as employment and transport, that directly affects disabled people.

The Equality Act 2010

The Equality Act 2010 prohibits discrimination against people with the protected characteristics that are specified in section 4 of the Act. Disability is one of the specified protected characteristics. Protection from discrimination for disabled people applies to disabled people in a range of circumstances, covering the provision of goods, facilities and services, the exercise of public functions, premises, work, education, and associations. Only those people who are defined as disabled in accordance with section 6 of the Act, and the associated Schedules and regulations made under that section, will be entitled to the protection that the Act provides to disabled people. However, importantly, the Act also provides protection for non-disabled people who are subjected to direct discrimination or harassment because of their association with a disabled person or because they are wrongly perceived to be disabled.

The Act defines a disabled person as, simply, a person with a disability. A person has a disability for the purposes of the Act if he or she has a physical or mental impairment and the impairment has a substantial and long-term adverse effect on his or her ability to carry out normal day-to-day activities

This means that, in general:

- o the person must have an impairment that is either physical or mental
- o the impairment must have adverse effects which are substantial
- o the substantial adverse effects must be long-term and
- o the long-term substantial adverse effects must have an effect on normal day-to-day activities

Definition of 'impairment'

The definition requires that the effects which a person may experience must arise from a physical or mental impairment. The term mental or physical impairment should be given its ordinary meaning. It is not necessary for the cause of the impairment to be established, nor does the impairment have to be the result of an illness. In many cases, there will be no dispute as to whether a person has an impairment. Any disagreement is more likely to be about whether the effects of the impairment are sufficient to fall within the definition and in particular whether they are long-term. This is a crucial fact.

Whether a person is disabled for the purposes of the Act is generally determined by reference to the effect that an impairment has on that person's ability to carry out normal day-to-day activities. An exception to this is a person with severe disfigurement. A disability can arise from a wide range of impairments which can be:

- sensory impairments, such as those affecting sight or hearing;
- impairments with fluctuating or recurring effects such as Rheumatoid arthritis, Myalgic encephalitis (ME), Chronic fatigue syndrome (CFS), Fibromyalgia, Depression and Epilepsy;
- progressive, such as Motor neurone disease, Muscular dystrophy, and forms of Dementia;
- auto-immune conditions such as Systemic lupus erythematosis (SLE);
- organ specific, including Respiratory conditions, such as Asthma, and cardiovascular diseases, including Thrombosis, Stroke and Heart disease;
- developmental, such as Autistic spectrum disorders (ASD), Dyslexia and Dyspraxia;
- learning disabilities;
- mental health conditions with symptoms such as anxiety, low mood, panic attacks, phobias, or unshared perceptions; eating disorders; bipolar affective disorders; obsessive compulsive disorders; personality disorders; post traumatic stress disorder, and some self-harming behaviour;
- Mental illnesses, such as depression and schizophrenia;
- produced by injury to the body, including to the brain.

Persons with HIV infection, cancer and multiple sclerosis

The Act states that a person who has cancer, HIV infection or Multiple sclerosis (MS) is a disabled person. This means that the person is protected by the Act effectively from the point of diagnosis.

Certain conditions are not regarded as impairments. These are:

- o addiction to, or dependency on, alcohol, nicotine, or any other substance (other than in consequence of the substance being medically prescribed);
- o the condition known as seasonal allergic rhinitis (e.g. hayfever), except where it aggravates the effect of another condition;
- o tendency to set fires;
- o tendency to steal;
- o tendency to physical or sexual abuse of other persons;
- o exhibitionism;

A person with an excluded condition may nevertheless be protected as a disabled person if he or she has an accompanying impairment which meets the requirements of the definition. For example, a person who is addicted to a substance such as alcohol may also have depression, or a physical impairment such as liver damage, arising from the alcohol addiction. While this person would not meet the definition simply on the basis of having an addiction, he or she may still meet the definition as a result of the effects of the depression or the liver damage.

Disfigurements which consist of a tattoo (which has not been removed), non-medical body piercing, or something attached through such piercing, are treated as not having a substantial adverse effect on the person's ability to carry out normal day-to-day activities.

The Act says that, except for the provisions in Part 12 (Transport) and section 190 (improvements to let dwelling houses), the provisions of the Act also apply in relation to a person who previously has had a disability as defined in the Act. This means that someone who is no longer disabled, but who met the requirements of the definition in the past, will still be covered by the Act. Also protected would be someone who continues to experience debilitating effects as a result of treatment for a past disability.

Definition of 'long-term effects'

The Act states that, for the purpose of deciding whether a person is disabled, a long-term effect of an impairment is one:

- which has lasted at least 12 months; or
- where the total period for which it lasts, from the time of the first onset, is likely to be at least 12 months; or
- which is likely to last for the rest of the life of the person affected

Special provisions apply when determining whether the effects of an impairment that has fluctuating or recurring effects are long-term. Also a person who is deemed to be a disabled person does not need to satisfy the long-term requirement.

The cumulative effect of related impairments should be taken into account when determining whether the person has experienced a long-term effect for the purposes of meeting the definition of a disabled person. The substantial adverse effect of an impairment which has developed from, or is likely to develop from, another impairment should be taken into account when determining whether the effect has lasted, or is likely to last at least twelve months, or for the rest of the life of the person affected.

Normal day-to-day activities

In general, day-to-day activities are things people do on a regular or daily basis, and examples include shopping, reading and writing, having a conversation or using the telephone, watching television, getting washed and dressed, preparing and eating food, carrying out household tasks, walking and travelling by various forms of transport, and taking part in social activities. Normal day-to-day activities can include general work-related activities, and study and education-related activities, such as interacting with colleagues, following instructions, using a computer, driving, carrying out interviews, preparing written documents, and keeping to a timetable or a shift pattern.

The term 'normal day-to-day activities' is not intended to include activities which are normal only for a particular person, or a small group of people. In deciding whether an activity is a normal day-to-day activity, account should be taken of how far it is carried out by people on a daily or frequent basis. In this context, 'normal' should be given its ordinary, everyday meaning.

A normal day-to-day activity is not necessarily one that is carried out by a majority of people. For example, it is possible that some activities might be carried out only, or more predominantly, by people of a particular gender, such as breast-feeding or applying make-up, and cannot therefore be said to be normal for most people. They would nevertheless be considered to be normal day-to-day activities.

Also, whether an activity is a normal day-to-day activity should not be determined by whether it is more normal for it to be carried out at a particular time of day. For example, getting out of bed and getting dressed are activities that are normally associated with the morning. They may be carried out much later in the day by workers who work night shifts, but they would still be considered to be normal day-to-day activities. The following examples demonstrate a range of day-to-day effects on impairment:

o Difficulty in getting dressed,
o Difficulty carrying out activities associated with toileting, or caused by frequent minor incontinence;
o Difficulty preparing a meal,
o Difficulty eating;

o Difficulty going out of doors unaccompanied, for example, because the person has a phobia, a physical restriction, or a learning disability;

o Difficulty waiting or queuing,

o Difficulty using transport; for example, because of physical restrictions, pain or fatigue, a frequent need for a lavatory or as a result of a mental impairment or learning disability;

o Difficulty in going up or down steps, stairs or gradients;

o A total inability to walk, or an ability to walk only a short distance without difficulty;

o Difficulty entering or staying in environments that the person perceives as strange or frightening;

o Behaviour which challenges people around the person, making it difficult for the person to be accepted in public places;

o Persistent difficulty crossing a road safely,

o Persistent general low motivation or loss of interest in everyday activities;

o Difficulty accessing and moving around buildings;

o Difficulty operating a computer, for example, because of physical restrictions in using a keyboard, a visual impairment or a learning disability;

o Difficulty picking up and carrying objects of moderate weight, such as a bag of shopping or a small piece of luggage, with one hand;

o Inability to converse, or give instructions orally, in the person's native spoken language;

o Difficulty understanding or following simple verbal instructions;

o Difficulty hearing and understanding another person speaking clearly over the voice telephone

- o Persistent and significant difficulty in reading or understanding written material where this is in the person's native written language,
- o Frequent confused behaviour, intrusive thoughts, feelings of being controlled, or delusions;
- o Persistently wanting to avoid people or significant difficulty taking part in normal social interaction or forming social relationships,
- o Persistent difficulty in recognising, or remembering the names of, familiar people such as family or friends;
- o Persistent distractibility or difficulty concentrating;
- o Compulsive activities or behaviour, or difficulty in adapting after a reasonable period to minor changes in a routine.

Whether a person satisfies the definition of a disabled person for the purposes of the Act will depend upon the full circumstances of the case. That is, whether the substantial adverse effect of the impairment on normal day-to-day activities is long term.

Specialised activities

Where activities are themselves highly specialised or involve highly specialised levels of attainment, they would not be regarded as normal day-to-day activities for most people. In some instances work-related activities are so highly specialised that they would not be regarded as normal day-to-day activities. The same is true of other specialised activities such as playing a musical instrument to a high standard of achievement; taking part in activities where very specific skills or level of ability are required; or playing a particular sport to a high level of ability, such as would be required for a professional footballer or athlete. Where activities involve highly specialised skills or levels of attainment, they would not be regarded as normal day-to-day activities for most people.

Normal day-to-day activities also include activities that are required to maintain personal well-being or to ensure personal safety, or the safety of other people. Account should be taken of whether the effects of an impairment have an impact on whether the person is inclined to carry out or neglect basic functions such as eating, drinking, sleeping, keeping warm or personal hygiene; or to exhibit behaviour which puts the person or other people at risk.

Indirect effects

An impairment may not directly prevent someone from carrying out one or more normal day-to-day activities, but it may still have a substantial adverse effect on how the person carries out those activities. For example pain or fatigue: where an impairment causes pain or fatigue, the person may have the ability to carry out a normal day-to-day activity, but may be restricted in the way that it is carried out because of experiencing pain in doing so. Or the impairment might make the activity more than usually fatiguing so that the person might not be able to repeat the task over a sustained period of time.

Disabled children

The effects of impairments may not be apparent in babies and young children because they are too young to have developed the ability to carry out activities that are normal for older children and adults. Regulations provide that an impairment to a child under six years old is to be treated as having a substantial and long-term adverse effect on the ability of that child to carry out normal day-to-day activities where it would normally have a substantial and long-term adverse effect on the ability of a person aged six years or over to carry out normal day-to-day activities.

Children aged six and older are subject to the normal requirements of the definition. That is, that they must have an impairment which has a substantial and long-term adverse effect on their ability to carry out normal day-to-day activities. However, in considering the ability of a child aged six or over to carry out a normal day-to-day activity, it is necessary to take account of the level of achievement which would be normal for a person of a similar age.

Part 6 of the Act provides protection for disabled pupils and students by preventing discrimination against them at school or in post-16 education because of, or for a reason related to, their disability. A pupil or student must satisfy the definition of disability as described in this guidance in order to be protected by Part 6 of the Act. The duties for schools in the Act, including the duty for schools to make reasonable adjustments for disabled children, are designed to dovetail with duties under the Special Educational Needs (SEN) framework which are based on a separate definition of special educational needs. Further information on these duties can be found in the SEN Code of Practice and the Equality and Human Rights Commission's Codes of Practice for Education.

****

Chapter 2

The Benefits System-What You Are Entitled To

As we have seen in Chapter 1, the Equality Act 2010 is central to every aspect of disability, and that includes benefits for disabled people.

Very often, disabled people are prevented from entering the workplace and earning a living, It follows that there will be a reliance on benefits to at least ensure a decent standard of living. In this chapter, we will be looking at the range of benefits available, including those benefits specifically aimed at disabled people and also benefits which are aimed at everyone. They cover everything which a disabled person might need to ensure that day to day living is taken care of. All rates quoted cover the year 2015-2016.

We will be looking at the following benefits:

- Attendance Allowance
- Personal Independence Payment
- Carers Allowance
- Housing Benefit
- Council Tax Support
- Pension Credit
- Income Support
- Job Seekers Allowance
- Employment and Support Allowance
- Universal Credit
- Tax Credits
- Winter Fuel payment

> ➢ Cold weather Payment
> ➢ TV Licence Concessions
> ➢ Bereavement Allowance

Attendance Allowance

You should be able to claim Attendance Allowance if your ability to look after your own personal care is affected by physical or mental illness or disability. Attendance Allowance has 2 weekly rates, and the rate you get very much depends on the help you need.

The current rates are:

- £55.10 if you need help in the day or at night
- £82.30 if you need help both in the day and at night.

Claiming Attendance Allowance won't affect any other income you receive, and it's also tax-free. If you are awarded it, you may become entitled to other benefits, such as Pension Credit, Housing Benefit or Council Tax Reduction, or an increase in these benefits.

You may be eligible for Attendance Allowance if you are 65 or over (if you're under 65, you may be eligible for Personal Independence Payment instead-see below), could benefit from help with personal care, such as getting washed or dressed, or supervision to keep you safe during the day or night, have any type of disability or illness, including sight or hearing impairments, or mental health issues such as dementia and have needed help for at least 6 months. (If you're terminally ill you can make a claim straight away.)

Attendance Allowance isn't means-tested, so your income and savings aren't taken into account. You don't actually have to receive help from a carer, as Attendance Allowance is based on the help you need, not the help you actually get. Also, you don't strictly have to spend your Attendance Allowance on care – it's up to you how you use it. You can get a claim form by calling the Attendance

Allowance helpline on 0845 605 6055 or 0345 605 6055 (textphone: 0845 604 5312). You can also download a claim form or claim online.

Attendance Allowance doesn't usually take into account problems with housework, cooking, shopping and gardening. If your application is turned down, ask an advice agency such as Citizens Advice about whether you should challenge the decision. Many applications are turned down because people don't mention or aren't clear about how their illness or disability affects their lives.

Personal Independence Payment

Personal Independence Payment (PIP) is a benefit for people of working age with disabilities. It has replaced Disability Living Allowance (DLA) for anyone making a new claim. If you're under 65 and already claiming DLA you'll eventually be asked to claim PIP instead. If you were 65 or over on 8 April 2013 and already claiming DLA, you won't be affected by the change and you'll continue to get DLA payments for as long as you're entitled to them.

You may be eligible for PIP if you're under 65 and need help with daily living activities or help getting around, or both. If you are 65 or over and you have care needs, you can't claim PIP but you may be able to claim Attendance Allowance. If you are awarded PIP before you are 65 it can continue after age 65. PIP isn't based on National Insurance contributions and isn't means-tested. You can claim it whether you're working or not.

Rates of Personal Independence Payment

PIP has two parts – a **daily living component** and a **mobility component.** They're paid at different rates, depending on the level of difficulty you have performing particular activities such as preparing food and drink or dressing and undressing. You may be able to claim one or both components.

Daily living component:

Standard rate - £55.10 per week
Enhanced rate - £82.30 per week

Mobility component:

Standard rate - £21.80 per week
Enhanced rate - £57.45 per week

To start your claim you'll need to call the Department for Work and Pensions (DWP) on 0800 917 2222 (textphone 0800 917 777). They will ask you for basic information and then send you a claim form. Most people will have to attend a face-to-face assessment of their needs as well. Find out more on the Gov.UK website. If your application is turned down contact an advice agency such as Citizens Advice about whether you should challenge the decision. Your needs may change and increase, so even if you're not eligible for PIP now, you may be able to claim successfully in the future.

Carer's Allowance

The main welfare benefit for carers is called Carer's Allowance and it's worth £62.10 per week if you're eligible. You don't have to be related to or live with the person you care for to claim Carer's Allowance. You'll also get National Insurance credits each week towards your pension if you're under pension age.

You may not think of yourself as a carer. Perhaps you've looked after someone for a long time without ever calling yourself one, or maybe you think the help you give your spouse or parent is simply what you should be doing. If so, you may have been missing out on the help that is available to you.

To claim Carer's Allowance, you must:

- spend at least 35 hours a week caring for a disabled person - you don't have to live with them
- care for someone who receives the higher- or middle-rate care component of Disability Living Allowance, either rate of Personal Independence Payment daily living component, or any rate of Attendance Allowance
- not earn more than £102 a week (after deductions)
- not be in full-time education.

Carer's Allowance may not be paid if you're receiving a State Pension or certain other benefits, but it's still worth claiming because you could get extra Pension Credit and/or Housing Benefit.

If you're claiming Universal Credit You may be able to get an extra amount because of your caring role without having to apply for Carer's Allowance. (see below for universal credit).

If you want to make a claim for carers allowance call the Carer's Allowance Unit on 0845 608 4321 (textphone: 0845 604 5312) to request a claim pack. Or you can visit GOV.UK to download a claim form or make a claim online.

Housing Benefit

Housing Benefit helps pay your rent if you are a tenant on a low income. It will not only reduce your rent but also cover some service charges like lifts and communal laundry facilities. How much you get depends on a number of factors:

- if you rent privately or from a council
- your household income and circumstances
- if you have empty rooms

You may receive more Housing Benefit if you get a disability or carer's benefit, such as Carer's Allowance, Attendance Allowance or Personal Independence Payment.

Housing Benefit is a means-tested benefit. The amount you can claim is affected by: your savings, who you live with, how much rent you pay and how many rooms you have in your home. If you get the Guarantee Credit part of Pension Credit you may get your rent paid in full by Housing Benefit. If you don't get Guarantee Credit - but have a low income and less than £16,000 in savings - you may still get some help.

You can't claim Housing Benefit if you own your own home. However, you may be eligible for Support with Mortgage Interest as part of Pension. If you're not claiming other benefits, you can get a claim form from your local council. You can apply for Housing Benefit at the same time as applying for Pension Credit. If you're already claiming Pension Credit, contact the Pension Service.

Council Tax Support

You may be eligible for Council Tax Support if you're on a low income or claim certain benefits. Council Tax Support replaced Council Tax Benefit in 2013, and each local authority now runs their own Council Tax Support schemes. Apply directly to your local council to see if you're entitled to support.

The support you get may depend on factors such as which benefits you receive, your age, your income, savings, who you live with and how much Council Tax you pay. If you receive a disability or carer's benefit, you may get more Council Tax Support. You may even get your Council Tax paid in full if you get the Guarantee Credit part of Pension Credit. If you don't get Guarantee Credit but have a low income and less than £16,000 in savings, you may still get some help. You can apply whether you own your home, rent, are working or currently unemployed.

Universal Credit

If you're of working age and making a new claim in an area where Universal Credit has been introduced, you should claim Universal

Credit to help with your rent. See below for more about Universal Credit.

Pension Credit

Pension Credit is an income-related benefit that comes in two parts and you may be eligible for one or both:

- Guarantee Credit tops up your weekly income to a guaranteed minimum level
- Savings Credit is extra money if you've got some savings or your income is higher than the basic State Pension

About 4 million older people are entitled to Pension Credit, yet about 1 in 3 of those eligible are still not claiming it. Don't be put off if you discover you're only eligible for a small amount of Pension Credit. It's your passport to other benefits, such as Housing Benefit and Council Tax Reduction.

Rates of Pension Credit

Guarantee Credit will top up your weekly income to:

- £151.20 if you're single
- or £230.85 if you're a couple.

If you qualify for Savings Credit, you can get up to:

- £14.82 extra per week if you're single
- or £17.43 if you're a couple.

Claiming Guarantee Credit

The minimum age to claim Guarantee Credit is gradually rising. In April 2015, it's 62 and a half years. If your weekly income is less than £151.20 if you're single, or £230.80 if you're a couple you may qualify for Guarantee Credit. If you have a disability, are a carer or have to pay housing costs, you may be eligible even if your income is higher than the amounts given above.

Claiming Savings Credit

If you're 65 or over you may also qualify for Savings Credit. There isn't a savings limit for Pension Credit, but if you have over £10,000 this will affect the amount you receive. Remember, you can claim one or both parts of Pension Credit.

Benefits of claiming Pension Credit

Pension Credit is also your passport to lots of other savings such as:

- It's unlikely you'll have to pay Council Tax (unless other people live with you).
- You'll get free NHS dental treatment, and you can claim help towards the cost of glasses and travel to hospital.
- You'll get a Cold Weather Payment of £25 when the temperature is 0°C or below for 7 days in a row.
- If you rent your home, you may get your rent paid in full by Housing Benefit.
- If you own your home, you may be eligible for help with mortgage interest, ground rent and service charges.
- If you're a carer, you may get an extra amount known as Carer Premium, or Carer Addition if it's paid with Pension Credit. This is worth up to £34.60 a week.

How make the claim

Call the Pension Credit claim line on 0800 99 1234 (textphone: 0800 169 0133).

Income Support

Income Support is a benefit for people under Pension Credit qualifying age and living on a low income. If you can't work for whatever reason or don't work many hours, you may get some support to top up your income. You can claim Income Support if you're all of the following:

- below the age you can claim Pension Credit
- a carer or, in some cases, if you're sick or disabled, or a single parent with a child under 5
- on a low income and have less than £16,000 in savings
- working fewer than 16 hours a week (if you have a partner they must work fewer than 24 hours a week).

If you qualify for Income Support, you could be entitled to other benefits, such as Housing Benefit or help with Council Tax, health costs or urgent one-off expenses.

Rates of Income support

- £73.10 a week if you're single
- £114.85 a week if you're a couple.

The amount you get may vary depending on your circumstances. For example you may get extra if you're a pensioner or if you're disabled. You can claim Income Support by phone. Contact Jobcentre Plus on 0800 055 6688 or textphone 0800 023 4888. Or you can you can fill out a claim form on GOV.UK. Print it out and post it to your local Jobcentre.

Jobseeker's Allowance

Jobseeker's Allowance is a taxable benefit to support people who are actively looking for work. To get Jobseeker's Allowance you must be either unemployed or working fewer than 16 hours a week.

If you're a couple and both out of work, you may have to make a joint claim.

There are 2 types of Jobseeker's Allowance:

- Contribution-based Jobseeker's Allowance pays £73.10 a week.

You can get this if you've paid enough National Insurance contributions over the last 2 years. It's paid for up to 6 months. You may get less if you have income from a part-time job or a private pension.

- Income-based Jobseeker's Allowance pays £73.10 a week if you're single and £114.85 a week if you're a couple.

The amount of income-based Jobseeker's Allowance you get may vary according to your age and whether you get disability or carer's benefits. It's means-tested so the amount you get will be affected by your savings. You can't get income-based Jobseeker's Allowance if you have over £16,000 in savings or if you or your partner works 24 or more hours a week.

To make a claim for Jobseeker's Allowance, contact your local Jobcentre Plus on 0800 055 6688 (textphone 0800 023 4888). You can also make a claim online on GOV.UK. When you make a claim, a Jobcentre Plus personal adviser will write out a Jobseeker's Agreement with you setting out the type of work you want and the steps you'll take to find a job. If your adviser feels you're not keeping to this agreement or if you pull out of a compulsory employment scheme, you can be sanctioned. This means your benefits could be reduced or stopped for a period.

Employment and Support Allowance

Employment and Support Allowance (ESA) is a benefit for people who are unable to work due to illness or disability. There are 2 types of ESA, and you may be entitled to one or both of them:

- Contribution-based ESA - you can get this if you've paid enough National Insurance contributions. It's taxable.
- Income-related ESA - you can get this if you have no income or a low income. You don't have to have paid National Insurance contributions and it isn't taxable.

During your claim you'll be called to 2 compulsory reviews, one after 13 weeks and the other after 26 weeks.

You can't claim income-related ESA if you claim Universal Credit or have savings of more than £16,000.

You'll have to attend a medical assessment called a 'work capability assessment'. You'll also have to fill in a 'limited capacity for work' questionnaire that looks at how your illness or disability affects what you do. After this you'll be told whether you're considered fit for work, or whether you're entitled to ESA.

If you are entitled to ESA, you'll be placed in the 'work-related activity group' or the 'support group'. People in the support group are exempt from the benefit cap. People in the work-related activity group get less money and are expected to prepare for an eventual return to the job market. If you don't, your benefit can be reduced for a period.

If you're entitled to income-related ESA, you may also qualify for other benefits such as Housing Benefit, Council Tax Reduction and help with health costs.

Rates of ESA
Income-related ESA
The amount of you get depends on your income and savings, whether you're single or a couple, whether you get disability or carer's benefits, and the result of your assessment. Income-related ESA can be paid on its own or as a top-up to contribution-based ESA.

Contribution-based ESA

You'll get a basic allowance of £73.10 for the first 13 weeks. After your assessment, you'll get: up to £102.15 a week if you're in the work-related activity group or up to £109.30 a week if you're in the support group. If you're in the work-related activity group, you'll get contribution-based ESA for one year; if you're in the support group, there's no time limit. Contribution-based ESA may be reduced if you have a private pension or you're claiming certain benefits.

To claim call Jobcentre Plus on 0800 055 6688 (textphone 0800 023 4888). They'll ask you questions over the phone and fill in the form for you. Or visit the GOV.UK website to download a claim form. Some benefits are means-tested. In other words, the amount of income and capital you have can affect your eligibility. Capital includes savings, investments, and property other than your own home.

Different means-testing rules apply, depending on whether you're under or over the minimum State Pension age. The information on this page only applies to people over the current minimum State Pension age (rising from 60 to 66 between 2010 and 2020). This information may also not apply to couples with one person under and the other over the minimum State Pension age.

Universal Credit

Universal Credit is a new benefit gradually being introduced nationally. It will eventually replace existing benefits:

- Income-based Jobseeker's Allowance
- Income-related Employment and Support Allowance
- Income Support
- Working Tax Credit
- Child Tax Credit

- Housing Benefit.

Who can get Universal Credit?

Universal Credit is gradually being rolled out across the UK, and it may not yet be available in the area where you live. To find out when Universal Credit will be rolled out in your area, contact Jobcentre Plus on 0800 055 6688 (textphone 0800 023 4888) or visit GOV.UK.

You may be able to claim Universal Credit if you're out of work or on a low income. If you qualify for other benefits such as contribution-based Jobseeker's Allowance or contribution-based Employment and Support Allowance, you should claim them as well as Universal Credit.

The amount of Universal Credit you get will depend on a number of factors, such as the amount of hours you work or how much savings you have. You can't get Universal Credit if you have savings of more than £16,000. Standard Universal Credit payments are:

- £317.82 per month if you're single
- £498.89 per month if you're a couple

You may be entitled to extra amounts if you have housing costs, caring responsibilities, dependent children

Claiming Universal Credit

You have to fill out an online claim form on GOV.UK. If you need help filling out the form, call the Universal Credit helpline on 0845 600 0723 (or textphone 0845 600 0743).Your online claim will be followed by a face-to-face interview.

When you make a claim you will have to agree to certain conditions in return for your benefit. This may be carrying out a training course, or agreeing to the number of hours you'll spend looking for work each week. This could be the case even if you're currently unable to work due to illness. If you don't meet the conditions, your benefit may be reduced.

Caps on all benefits

The government has imposed a cap on the amount of benfits an inividual or couple/family can receive over the course of a year. The cap applies to the total amount that the people in your household get from the following benefits:

- Bereavement Allowance
- Carer's Allowance
- Child Benefit
- Child Tax Credit
- Employment and Support Allowance (unless you get the support component)
- Guardian's Allowance
- Housing Benefit
- Incapacity Benefit
- Income Support
- Jobseeker's Allowance
- Maternity Allowance
- Severe Disablement Allowance
- Widowed Parent's Allowance (or Widowed Mother's Allowance or Widows Pension you started getting before 9 April 2001)

The level of the cap is:
- £500 a week for couples (with or without children living with them)
- £500 a week for single parents whose children live with them

- £350 a week for single adults who don't have children, or whose children don't live with them

This may mean the amount you get for certain benefits will go down to make sure that the total amount you get isn't more than the cap level.

Who won't be affected?

You might still be affected by the cap if you have any grown-up children or non-dependants who live with you and they qualify for one of the benefits below. This is because they won't normally count as part of your household.

You're not affected by the benefit cap if anyone in your household qualifies for Working Tax Credit or gets any of the following benefits:

- Disability Living Allowance
- Personal Independence Payment
- Attendance Allowance
- Industrial Injuries Benefits (and equivalent payments as part of a war disablement pension or the Armed Forces Compensation Scheme)
- Employment and support allowance if you get the support component
- War Widow's or War Widower's Pension
- War pensions
- Armed Forces Compensation Scheme
- Armed Forces Independence Payment

Tax credits

At the time of writing, the government is actively thinking of reducing tax credit payments. However, for the moment they are still available. You should keep an eye on the proposed changes.

Working Tax Credit

You can get Working Tax Credit if you or your partner are working enough hours a week and your income is low enough. You don't need to have children to qualify. You must be living in the UK.

The number of hours a week you have to work to be able to get Working Tax Credit depends on your circumstances. If you're single or in a couple, and have no children, you can qualify if: you are 25 or over and you work at least 30 hours a week, or you are 16 or over and you work at least 16 hours a week and you are disabled and you get a qualifying benefit, or you are 60 or over and you work at least 16 hours a week.

If you're single and have at least one child, you can qualify if you are 16 or over and you work at least 16 hours a week and you are responsible for a child or young person.

Working Tax Credits and children

If you are responsible for a child or young person, you can get Working Tax Credit provided you work at least 16 hours a week if you're single, or at least 24 hours between you if you're in a couple, with one of you working at least 16 hours a week. Some couples with children may qualify without working for 24 hours between them, provided one of them works 16 hours. Your income also needs to be low enough. A child is someone under 16, and a young person is someone who is 16, 17, 18 or 19 and still in full-time education up to A level or equivalent, or on certain approved training courses. You are responsible for a child or young person if they normally live with you or you have main responsibility for their care. You cannot usually get Working Tax Credit if your child is in local authority care.

You may be able to get Working Tax Credit for a short period after your child is 16 or leaves school, depending on when their birthday is and what they do on leaving school.

If you are on maternity leave, paternity leave or adoption leave and you normally work 16 hours or more, you can claim Working Tax Credit before you go back to work, as long as you are responsible for a child. If it is your first baby and you are not responsible for any other children, you will have to wait until the child is born, or comes to live with you before you can claim.

Working Tax Credit and disability

You can get Working Tax Credit if you are disabled provided you work at least 16 hours a week and your income is low enough and you get certain benefits because of your disability and your disability puts you at a disadvantage in getting a job.

The qualifying benefits include Incapacity Benefit, Disability Living Allowance, Personal Independence Payment, Armed Forces Independence Payment, Employment and Support Allowance, Attendance Allowance, Industrial Injuries Disablement Benefit, Statutory Sick Pay, a war pension with constant attendance allowance, occupational sick pay or Income Support or National Insurance credits awarded because you have been unable to work. There are rules about how long you have to have been getting some of these benefits before you claim Working Tax Credit. Some of these benefits stop once you are working, and some carry on.

Income levels and Working Tax Credits

Even if you meet the work conditions, you will only get Working Tax Credit if you have a low enough income. Your income for tax credits is assessed on an annual basis. Whether or not you get Working Tax Credit, and how much you get, depends on your income and your circumstances. Not all your income will be taken into account (for example, maintenance and child support, most Statutory Maternity, Paternity or Adoption Pay and all Maternity Allowance paid to you is ignored). Usually, HM Revenue and

Customs (HMRC) will use your income for the previous tax year to work out what you are due.

Working Tax Credit rates

The maximum Working Tax Credit you can get is calculated by adding together different elements which are based on your circumstances. There is a basic element which is included for anyone who is entitled to Working Tax Credit. There is a second adult element if you are claiming as a member of a couple although there are some circumstances where a couple will not get this. You have to claim as a couple if you live with a partner. This includes a partner of the opposite or same sex. There is a lone parent element if you are a lone parent.

There is a 30 hour element if you work at least 30 hours a week (or if you are claiming as a couple with a child and you jointly work at least 30 hours). There is a disability element if you are disabled, get certain benefits and you work at least 16 hours a week. You can also get a disability element if your partner qualifies for it or two disability elements if you both qualify.

There is a severe disability element if you get the highest rate care component of Disability Living Allowance, the enhanced rate of the daily living component of Personal Independence Payment, the higher rate of Attendance Allowance, or Armed Forces Independence Payment. You will get two severe disability elements if you and your partner both qualify.

You may also be able to get a childcare element. This is equivalent to up to 70% of childcare costs provided by a registered childminder, out-of-school club or another approved provider. There is a limit on the maximum eligible weekly childcare cost which means that the most this element can be is 70% of the maximum.

Rates of Working Tax Credit

Element of Working Tax Credit	Maximum annual amount from 6 April 2014	Maximum annual amount from 6 April 2015
Basic element	£1,940	£1,960
Second adult element	£1,990	£2,010
Lone parent element	£1,990	£2,010
30 hour element	£800	£810
Disability element	£2,935	£2,970
Severe disability element	£1,255	£1,275

Childcare element (up to 70% of the maximum):	Maximum weekly amount from 6 April 2014	Maximum weekly amount from 6 April 2015
Maximum weekly eligible cost for one child	£175 (maximum payable £122)	£175 (maximum payable £122)
Maximum weekly eligible cost for two or more children	£300 (maximum payable £210)	£300 (maximum payable £210)

Calculating Working Tax Credit

To work out how much Working Tax Credit is due, the separate elements of Working Tax Credit which apply to you are added together. If you are entitled to Child Tax Credit as well as Working Tax Credit, your maximum Child Tax Credit is worked out at the same time and added to your maximum Working Tax Credit.

Your income for the tax year is compared to a threshold of £6,420. Usually, your income for the previous tax year is used. If your income is less than the threshold, you get the maximum Working Tax Credit (and Child Tax Credit if this applies). If your income is more than the threshold, your tax credit will be reduced. Working Tax Credit (except for the childcare element) is taken away first, followed by the childcare element. If your income is too high, you will not get any Working Tax Credit. However, you may still get some Child Tax Credit, if you are entitled, because this is the last part of your total tax credits to be reduced.

To apply for Working Tax Credit, contact the Tax Credit helpline for an application pack. The application form for your first claim is Form TC600. The helpline number is 0345 300 3900 (textphone 0345 300 3909).

When you apply for Working Tax Credit, you will have to provide your national insurance number. You will normally also have to give the national insurance number of any partner who lives with you. If you don't know your national insurance number, but you think you have one, try to provide information that will help the office find your number. If you do not have a national insurance number, you will have to apply for one.

You may be able to get some Working Tax Credit for a period before you apply, if you met the conditions and could have claimed earlier. You can normally only get Working Tax Credit backdated for a maximum of 31 days before the date you apply.

How is Working Tax Credit paid

Working Tax Credit can be paid directly into your bank or building society account, or into a post office card account. If you do not give your account details to HM Revenue and Customs (HMRC), you may lose your entitlement to Working Tax Credit. If you have difficulties opening an account, you should get in touch with HMRC and explain.

Tax credits are awarded for a complete tax year. A tax year runs from 6 April one year to 5 April the next year. If you claim after April, your award will run from the date you claim to the end of the tax year. The amount you get is usually set for a year. If your circumstances change during the period of your award you should tell HMRC as soon as possible. This is important because otherwise you may not be paid all the tax credit you are entitled to or you may be paid too much and have to pay it back to HMRC.   Some changes to your circumstances mean that your award ends and you have to claim again. Other changes mean that your award continues but it will be recalculated, and some will not affect your current award at all.

Shortly after the end of the tax year, HMRC will send you an annual review pack which may ask you to give them further information. They call this a renewal pack. However, it's very important that you provide any information requested, even if you don't want to renew your claim, because HMRC will use this to finalise your award for the year just ended. If you don't reply when asked to do so, your payments will stop and you may have to pay back an overpayment.

If your work ends, you can carry on getting Working Tax Credit for a further four weeks. This also applies if you start to work less than 16 hours a week, or in some cases, less than 30 hours a week.

If you are refused Working Tax Credit and think you are entitled, or that the amount you are awarded is wrong, call the Tax Credits Helpline and ask HM Revenue and Customs (HMRC) to explain their decision. If you are not satisfied with the explanation, you can make a formal request for the decision to be looked at again. This is called a mandatory reconsideration. You must ask for a reconsideration within 30 days of the date of the decision. If you are not satisfied with the result of the reconsideration, you can then appeal to an independent tribunal.

It's against the law for you to be treated unfairly because of your race, sex, disability, sexuality, religion or belief when HMRC decide about your Working Tax Credit claim. Also, HMRC has a policy which says they will not discriminate against you because of other things, such as if you've got HIV or if you have caring responsibilities. If you feel that you've been discriminated against, you can make a complaint about this.

Other help when you get Working Tax Credit

When you get Working Tax Credit, you may be entitled to other financial help. If you pay rent, you may be able to get Housing Benefit. If you have to pay Council Tax, you may be able to get Council Tax Reduction. Being on Working Tax Credit may also give you access to other help. For example, you may be entitled to health benefits, including free prescriptions. You may also be able get help with the costs of a new baby from a Sure Start maternity grant or help with the costs of a funeral from a funeral payment. Whether or not you can get this help will depend on your income, whether you get a disability element with your Working Tax Credit and whether you also get Child Tax Credit.

Winter Fuel Payment

Winter Fuel Payment or Winter Fuel Allowance is an annual payment to help with heating costs, made to households with someone over Pension Credit age. Not heating homes properly puts people at risk of cold-related illnesses such as a heart attack or even hypothermia. The rates for winter fuel payment currently are £200 if you're under 80 and £300 if you're 80 or over

In winter 2015-16, you will qualify for the payment if you were born before 5 January 1953.

You only need to claim once. After this, you should get it automatically each year, as long as your circumstances do not change. The payment is made directly into your bank account in November or December. For more information you should call the Winter Fuel Payments Helpline on 0845 915 1515.

Cold Weather Payment

Cold Weather Payments are made to eligible people when the weather is very cold. You get £25 a week when the average temperature has been, or is expected to be, 0°C or below for 7 days in a row (between 1 November and 31 March).

You automatically receive the payment, if you get Pension Credit or certain other means-tested benefits. If you think that you are entitled to a cold weather payment and don't get one contact the Pension Service.

TV licence concessions

You could be entitled to a concession for a TV licence if you are over 75 or someone who is over 75 lives with you. You could also be entitled if you are registered as blind or severely sight impaired or are retired or disabled and live in certain accommodation

The TV licence for your main home doesn't cover you if you have a second home. You will have to buy a separate licence. If you have a licence for your main home, you won't need another if you have a static caravan or mobile home and you don't use the TV at the same time in both places.

You need to apply for a free TV licence if you're 75 or over as it's not given out automatically. You'll need to provide your date of birth and National insurance number (or a photocopy of your passport, driving licence or birth certificate). If you share your house with someone younger than 75, you can still apply for a free licence but it must be in your name. You can apply for your concession by calling 0300 790 6165 or visiting the TV licensing website. Once you have your free TV licence, it will renew automatically annually.

If you apply for a TV licence and you are 74 when you renew your licence you can apply for a short term licence until you are 75.

Concessions for blind and sight-impaired

If you're blind or severely sight-impaired, you can claim a 50% discount on your TV licence. When you apply, you'll need to provide a photocopy of the certificate from your local authority or ophthalmologist confirming your status as well as your TV licence application form and fee. Once you're registered, all your TV licence renewals will be at the concessionary rate.

If you live with someone who is blind or severely-sight impaired, you can get the 50% discount if you transfer the TV licence to the name of that person. You can apply for your concession by calling 0300 790 6165 or visiting the TV licensing website. If you've already paid the TV licence fee but qualify for the blind concession, fill out the TV Licensing online refund form.

Care homes and sheltered housing

You may be entitled to a TV licence concession if you live in a care home or sheltered housing. This licence is called an Accommodation for Residential Care (ARC) licence and it costs £7.50. You'll only need to get one if you watch TV in your own separate accommodation, not if you only watch it in common areas such as a residents' lounge. To qualify, you must be retired and aged 60 or over or disabled and live in accommodation which is eligible. If you think you qualify, contact the warden, staff or managing authority where you live. They will apply for one for you.

If you've already paid your full licence fee and now qualify for an ARC licence, ask your care home manager to help you apply for a refund. If you have questions about the ARC licence, phone TV licensing on 0300 790 6011 or visit the TV licensing website.

Bereavement allowance

Bereavement benefits include:

- o Bereavement Payment - a one-off lump sum you claim when your spouse or civil partner dies
- o Widowed Parent's Allowance if you have dependent Bereavement Allowance if you don't have dependent children

Bereavement benefits are paid to widows, widowers or the surviving partner of a civil partnership. You can get a bereavement benefit if your husband, wife or civil partner died on or after 9 April 2001. If you are a man whose wife died before this date, you may still be able to get some benefit.

You can get a bereavement benefit if you were legally married to your husband or wife who has now died. You can also get a bereavement benefit if you and your same-sex partner who has died registered a civil partnership.

You can't get any of the bereavement benefits if you were divorced from your husband or wife when they died, or you and your civil partner had dissolved your civil partnership. You are also excluded from claiming bereavement benefits if you remarry, or register another civil partnership. If you are getting a bereavement benefit when you remarry or register another civil partnership, it will stop. Even if you do not remarry or register another civil partnership, you cannot get bereavement benefits if you live with another partner. You can't get bereavement benefits in prison.

Bereavement Payment

A Bereavement Payment is a one-off tax-free lump sum payment of £2,000. You can claim it if you were widowed on or after 9 April 2001. You must claim within twelve months of your husband's, wife's or civil partner's death, unless there are exceptional circumstances which mean that you did not know about the death or it was not confirmed.

You are entitled to a Bereavement Payment if your husband, wife, or civil partner who has died paid enough national insurance contributions. If they died as the result of an industrial accident or an industrial disease, it does not matter whether they paid enough contributions or not.

To get Bereavement Payment you must have been below state pension age when your husband, wife or civil partner died, or - if you were over state pension age - they must not have been entitled to state retirement pension, based on their own national insurance contributions, when they died. You must have been married to your husband or wife, or in a registered civil partnership with your partner when they died. Until 6 April 2010, state pension age was 60 for a woman and 65 for a man. Since this date, the minimum age at which both men and women can claim a state pension is gradually being set to age 65 and will be increased, depending on which year you were born.

In England and Wales, you can claim a Bereavement Payment and tell the DWP about the death at the same time, by calling the DWP Bereavement Service on:

Telephone: 0845 606 0265
Textphone: 0845 606 0285
Telephone: 0845 606 0275 (Welsh)
Textphone: 0845 606 0295 (Welsh)

The Bereavement Service can take your claim for bereavement benefits over the phone and do a benefits check to see if you qualify for any other benefits as a result of the death.

Widowed Parent's Allowance

Widowed Parent's Allowance is a weekly payment made to a widow, widower or surviving civil partner with dependent children. Your husband, wife or civil partner must usually have died on or after 9 April 2001. However, if you are a man and your wife died before this date, you were under 65 when she died and you did not re-marry before 9 April 2001, you can also claim Widowed Parent's Allowance.

You can get Widowed Parent's Allowance if you are bringing up a child or you are a woman expecting your husband's baby. You can also get Widowed Parent's Allowance if you are a woman who was living with your civil partner when she died and you are pregnant as a result of fertility treatment.

If you are bringing up a child you must usually be getting Child Benefit for that child. The child should be:

o   the child of you and your late spouse, or
o   the child of you and your late civil partner, or
o   a child who you or your late spouse or civil partner got Child Benefit for at the time of your spouse or civil partner's death (for example, it could be your adopted child or a step-child).

You must have been under state pension age when your husband, wife or civil partner died, and your spouse or civil partner must have paid enough national insurance contributions for you to get Widowed Parent's Allowance. The only exception is if their death was caused by an industrial injury or an industrial disease, when it does not matter if enough national insurance contributions had been paid. If you need more information about the contribution conditions for Widowed Parent's Allowance, you should consult an experienced adviser, for example, at a Citizens Advice Bureau.

The amount of the basic Widowed Parent's Allowance will depend on your late husband, wife or civil partner's national insurance contributions, unless they died because of an industrial injury or disease.

In England and Wales, you can report the death and claim Widowed Parent's Allowance by calling the Department for Work and Pensions (DWP) Bereavement Service. They will take a claim for bereavement benefits over the phone. In Northern Ireland, call the Social Security Agency Bereavement Service.

In the same phone call, the DWP can also do a benefits check to see if you qualify for any other benefits as a result of the death. Alternatively, you can claim Widowed Parent's Allowance on form BB1. You can get form BB1 from your local Jobcentre Plus office or, in England, Wales and Scotland, from the GOV.UK website at www.gov.uk or by calling Jobcentre Plus on:

Freephone: 0800 055 6688
Textphone: 0800 023 4888
Welsh language line: 0800 012 1888

You should claim Widowed Parent's Allowance within three months of the date of death, to avoid losing any money. If you claim later than this, your benefit can only be backdated for up to three months

If you claim late, you can ask for backdating on the claim form. You do not have to give a reason for claiming late as long as you can show that you were entitled to Widowed Parent's Allowance before you made your claim. In some cases, you may be able to get Widowed Parent's Allowance for more than three months before you made your claim.

You can get Widowed Parent's Allowance until you stop getting Child Benefit. If this happens within 52 weeks of your husband, wife or civil partner's death, you can claim Bereavement Allowance for the rest of the 52 weeks.

Widow's pension

Widow's Pension is paid until you are 65, when you become entitled to a Retirement Pension at the same rate as the Widow's Pension. If you are over state pension age (60) but under 65, you can choose to stay on Widow's Pension or claim Retirement Pension.

Payments for funeral expenses

If you have to pay for a funeral for your partner, a close relative or friend, you may be able to claim a funeral payment from the Social Fund. Partners include lesbian, gay and heterosexual partners, whether you were married, in a civil partnership or living together. To get a funeral payment, you must be getting Income Support, income-based Jobseeker's Allowance, income-related Employment and Support Allowance, Pension Credit, Universal Credit or Housing Benefit. Some people getting Child Tax Credit or Working Tax Credit may also be entitled to a funeral payment.

Financial help if your husband, wife or civil partner was in the Armed Forces

If your husband, wife or civil partner died as a result of serving in the Armed Forces, you may be able to get financial help from the Service Personnel and Veterans Agency (SPVA). It does not matter whether your husband, wife or civil partner died during active service or not, as long as the death was caused by service in the Armed Forces. You may get a War Widow's or War Widower's pension, or a guaranteed income payment (based on your spouse or civil partner's earnings), depending on when the injury, illness or death was caused.

For information on benefits arising from work related injuries and illnesses see Chapter 4 Employment Rights.

****

Ch. 3

The Criminal Injuries Compensation Scheme 2012

The Criminal Injuries Compensation Scheme is a government funded scheme designed to compensate blameless victims of violent crime in Great Britain. The Criminal Injuries Compensation Authority (CICA), administer the Scheme and decide all claims. The rules of the Scheme and the value of the payments awarded are set by Parliament and are calculated by reference to a tariff of injuries.

You do not need a paid representative such as a solicitor or claims management company to apply for compensation. Free independent advice should be available from Victim Support or other charitable organisations. Victim Support is an independent national charity for people affected by crime and gives free and confidential support, and practical help to victims and witnesses of crime. This can include helping you with your claim, although they cannot provide legal advice. You can contact them by:

o telephoning the Victim Support line on 0845 30 30 900 (England and Wales) or 0845 60 39 213 (Scotland);
o visiting their website at www.victimsupport.org.uk or www.victimsupportsco.org.uk; or
o emailing supportline@victimsupport.org.uk or info@victimsupportsco.org.uk

You can also get advice from your local Citizens Advice service, a law centre, or from a welfare rights organisation. If you belong to a trade union, they may be able to help.

Paid representation and other help

If you choose paid representation you will have to pay these costs yourself. Where someone is representing you on a 'no-win no-fee' basis this usually means that they will keep a share of your payment to cover their fees. You can also ask a friend or a relative to represent you and help you make a claim.

Payments available from the Scheme

Claims can be considered for the following:

o   mental or physical injury following a crime of violence;
o   sexual or physical abuse;
o   loss of earnings - where you have no or limited capacity to work as the direct result of a criminal injury;
o   special expenses payments - these cover certain costs you may have incurred as a direct result of an incident. You can only ask them to consider special expenses if your injuries mean you have been unable to work or have been incapacitated to a similar extent for more than 28 weeks;
o   a fatality caused by a crime of violence including bereavement payments, payments for loss of parental services and financial dependency; and funeral payments.

The Hardship Fund

If your injuries are not serious enough to fall within the tariff of injuries, the Government has introduced a Hardship Fund. The Hardship Fund provides temporary relief from financial hardship to very low paid workers who are temporarily unable to work because they have been a victim of a violent crime. The fund only applies to injuries sustained in England and Wales. For more information, you should contact the Victim Support line on 0845 3030 900.

Making an application for payment

The Compensation Scheme may ask for evidence that you have:

- considered if it was possible to claim compensation from your assailant and pursued this if there was a chance of success;
- asked your employer about damages or insurance entitlements; and
- applied for all benefits to which you may be entitled.

You may still be eligible for an award under the Scheme even if your assailant is not known, or is not convicted.

You must apply as soon as it is reasonably practicable for you to do so. If you were an adult at the time of the incident, this should normally not be later than two years after it occurred. The limit can only be extended where:

- due to exceptional circumstances an application could not have been made earlier; and
- the evidence provided in support of the application means that it can be determined without further extensive enquiries by a claims officer.

The decision will be based on the 'balance of probabilities' which is different from a criminal court which decides on the basis of 'beyond reasonable doubt'. The scheme do not need to wait for the outcome of a criminal trial if there is already enough information to make a decision on your case.

If you wish the scheme to consider your application more than two years from the date of the incident you will need to provide evidence that shows why this application could not have been made earlier. You must also be able to provide supporting evidence for your claim that means that the claims officer can make a decision without further extensive enquiries.

Time limit for applicants under 18 years of age on the date of the incident

Special provision is made in the Scheme if you were under 18 at the time of the incident. Although they will consider later applications from you in those circumstances, it is best if you apply as soon as possible. If you are not able to make your own application, your parent or guardian can apply on your behalf. If an application is made close to the time of the incident it will be easier for you to provide evidence that you were injured as the result of a crime of violence.

If the incident or period of abuse was reported to the police before you turned 18, and no-one made a claim on your behalf, you can make a claim up until the day of your 20th birthday. If the incident or period of abuse took place before you turned 18, but was not reported to the police at the time, you can apply within two years from you reporting the incident or abuse to the police. If you wish the scheme to extend these periods for applying you will also need to provide them with evidence that shows why the application could not have been made earlier.

You can apply for compensation online. If you have no access to online services or need help to complete your application, the Customer Service Centre advisors on 0300 003 3601 can help.

Applying on behalf of children

If you are the parent, or person with parental responsibility for a child, you can complete an application on their behalf. You will be asked to provide your details and proof of your relationship to the child.

Applying on behalf of an adult who cannot apply themselves

If you have the authority to act on behalf of a person who lacks the capacity to make their own application, you can apply on their behalf. The scheme will seek evidence that you are entitled to act on their behalf.

They may also need you to obtain medical evidence that the person you are representing lacks capacity, or is 'incapable by reason of mental disorder', within the meanings of the Mental Capacity Act 2005 (England and Wales) or Adults with Incapacity (Scotland) Act 2000.

If the person does not already have someone who is legally appointed to act on their behalf, then you could consider applying to the Court of Protection in England and Wales for the appointment of a deputy or for a single order or, in Scotland, to the Sheriff Court for the appointment of a financial welfare guardian or for an intervention order. There is more information at www.publicguardian.gov.uk (England and Wales) or www.publicguardian-scotland.gov.uk (Scotland).

If you are injured outside Great Britain

If you are a United Kingdom (UK) resident and were injured as a result of a crime of violence in another country which is part of the European Union (EU) the scheme can help you apply for compensation from that country. You should call the EU Assistance Team on 0300 003 3061 or email eucat@cica.gsi.gov.uk. Details of compensation schemes in other countries can be found on the EU Judicial website

If you were injured outside the EU, you may be able to apply under a similar scheme operated by the country concerned. You should contact the Foreign and Commonwealth Office for more information. Details can be found on www.gov.uk.

If you were injured in Northern Ireland, you should contact Compensation Services at:

Compensation Services
Sixth Floor

Millennium House
25 Great Victoria Street
Belfast
BT2 7AQ
Telephone: 0300 200 7887.

If you were ordinarily resident in the UK and you were injured outside the UK in a terrorist attack, you may be able to claim under the Victims of Overseas Terrorism Compensation Scheme. Please see the compensation scheme website for more information at www.gov.uk.

The Criminal Injuries Compensation Scheme at ww.gov.uk offers detailed information about claiming for compensation and the criteria involved.

****

Chapter 4

Carers and Help For Carers

In chapter 2, we looked at the range of benefits available to disabled people, including Carers Allowance.

In this chapter, we will look at the all important role of a carer in the life of a disabled person. This section, although meant for carers, will also be of benefit to a disabled person who wishes to know more about the caring profession and what this entails.

What is a Carer?

A carer is anyone who cares, unpaid, for a friend or family member who due to illness, disability, a mental health problem or an addiction cannot cope without their support. The causes of someone taking on caring responsibilities include:

o   Serious physical illness
o   Long-term physical disability
o   Long-term neurological conditions
o   Mental health problems
o   Dementia
o   Addiction
o   Learning difficulties

The variety of tasks that a carer fulfils is diverse. They can include practical household tasks such as cooking, cleaning, washing up, ironing, paying bills and financial management, personal care such as bathing, dressing, lifting, administering medication and collecting prescriptions and emotional support.

Although the distinction is often made between a full-time or part-time carer, there is not a minimum time requirement or age restriction that "qualifies" someone as being more or less of a carer. If you provide care and support to an adult friend or family member, you may be eligible for support from your local council. Examples might be someone suffering from dementia or mental illness.

This support could include being offered money to pay for things that make caring easier. Or the local authority might offer practical support, such as arranging for someone to step in when you need a short break. It could also put you in touch with local support groups so you have people to talk to.

The Care Act 2014

The Care Act 2014, which was given Royal assent in May 2014, makes carer's assessments more widely available to people in caring roles. Local authorities now have a legal duty to assess any carer who requests one or who appears to need support. If you are a carer and you need some support, you should get in touch with the council covering the area where the person you care for lives. The council will provide you with information and advice about how the assessment will work.

Essentially, a Carer's assessment is a discussion between you and a trained person either from the council or another organisation that the council works with. The assessment will consider the impact the care and support you provide is having on your own wellbeing, as well as important aspects of the rest of your life, including the things you want to achieve day-to-day. It must also consider other important issues, such as whether you are able or willing to carry on caring, whether you work or want to work, and whether you want to study or do more socially. The assessment can be carried out face-to-face, over the telephone or online.

Eligibility for care and support services

A carer's assessment looks at the different ways caring affects your life, and works out how you can carry on doing the things that are important to you and your family. It covers your caring role, your feelings about caring, your physical, mental and emotional health, and how caring affects your work, leisure, education, wider family and relationships. Your physical, mental and emotional wellbeing should be at the heart of this assessment.

When the assessment is complete, the local authority will decide whether your needs are "eligible" for support from the local authority. After the assessment, they will write to you about their decision and give you reasons to explain what they have decided. If you have eligible needs, your council will contact you to discuss what help might be available. If you do not have needs that are eligible, your council will give you information and advice, including what local care and support is available. This could include, for example, help from local voluntary organisations.

Before the assessment

If you have arranged to have a carer's assessment of your needs, give yourself time to think about your role as a carer. You should consider:

- whether you want to continue being a carer
- if you were prepared to continue, what changes would make your life easier
- if there is any risk that you will not be able to continue as a carer without support
- whether you have any physical or mental health problems, including stress or depression, which make your role as a carer more difficult
- whether being a carer affects your relationships with other people, including family and friends

- o if you are in paid work, whether being a carer causes problems at your work (such as often being late)
- o if you like more time to yourself so that you can have a rest or enjoy some leisure activity
- o if you like to do some training, voluntary work or paid work

When your carer's assessment is done, you can then consider:

- o whether to be a carer at all
- o how much care you are willing to provide
- o the type of care you are willing to provide

It is vital that the assessment considers whether the role of a carer is affecting your health or safety. Carers sometimes take on physical tasks, such as lifting and carrying, which can cause long-term health problems. Others can find that the stress of the role can lead to depression or other mental health problems. In some cases, safety can be an issue; for instance, because of the behaviour of the person they look after.

- o During your assessment, explain any mental or physical health problems you are experiencing. Social services will consider all aspects of your health and safety, including caring tasks that might put your health or wellbeing at risk.

One of the most important parts of the carer's assessment will be a discussion about your wishes concerning paid work, training or leisure activities. The local authority must consider the support you may need if you want to stay in your paid job or return to paid work. They must also consider the support you may need if you want to continue or start studying or training.

If you are looking after someone, the local authority will consider a broad range of issues that can affect your ability to provide care as part of their assessment of your needs. When assessing your needs, social services must consider whether your role as a carer is sustainable. The assessment is about your needs and therefore you should:

- have a reasonably detailed discussion about all the matters relevant to you
- have the assessment in private if you want to, at a convenient time and place for you
- get relevant information, including about welfare benefits you could claim and details of other services
- have a chance to identify the outcomes that you want; any services should be appropriate for you and meet your needs
- be given flexibility and innovation in identifying services that may meet your needs
- have an opportunity to give feedback about the assessment
- be told about any charges before services are arranged

After your assessment, you and the local authority will agree a support plan, which sets out how your needs will be met. This might include help with housework, buying a laptop to keep in touch with family and friends, or becoming a member of a gym so you can look after their own health.

Your support plan should consider whether your situation is likely to change, but you may want to contact social services and ask them to reassess you if this happens.

Parent carer assessments

If you are a parent of a disabled child aged under 18, your child can be assessed by the local authority under law relating to the needs of children in the Children and Families Act 2014. You will also be assessed as part of that process because social services will look at the needs of the family as a whole. This is often referred to as a "holistic" assessment.

The assessment should take into account detailed information about your family, including:

- o   the family's background and culture
- o   your own views and preferences
- o   the needs of any other children you have
- o   The assessment is not a test of your parenting skills, but should be a sensitive look at any difficulties the family has as a whole, with a view to considering what support or services are needed.

A care plan should be drawn up that would include services to benefit both you and your disabled child. For example, there could be adaptations to the home, help with bathing or regular respite breaks to ensure you get the rest you need. You could also choose to have a direct payment so that you can buy in your own services for your child.

Hospital discharge and NHS continuing care

You might have a carer's assessment or a review of your support plan if the person you care for has been in hospital and is being discharged.

As well as care and support organised by the council, some people are also eligible to receive help from the NHS. This help may be a nursing service for people who are ill or recovering at home after leaving hospital. It could include things like changing the dressings on wounds or giving medication. If you are eligible for this kind of help, a health professional such as your GP or community nurse should be able to tell you.

In exceptional circumstances, where an adult has a complex medical condition and substantial ongoing care needs, the NHS provides a service called NHS continuing healthcare. NHS continuing healthcare provides care and support in a person's home, care home or hospice.

****

.

Chapter 5

Options for Care-Paying for Care Homes

In this chapter, we will cover the range of issues covering care homes and the decision to move into a care home. Whether or not you need care home provision will depend on a range of factors, not least the extent of your disability. One of the first and most important options you will have to consider when choosing residential care is whether you need the care home to provide nursing care, or just standard personal care.

There are a variety of options available, from permanent care homes for older people, homes for younger adults with disabilities, and homes for children. Care homes may be privately owned or run by charities or councils. Some will be small care homes based in home-like domestic dwellings, while others will be based in large communal centres.

Options for care before choosing a care home

Going into a care home is a major commitment– it involves changing where you live and potentially committing to paying a considerable amount of money for your ongoing accommodation and care needs. Before you decide to move to a care home, you should think about other options, including:

- o   home care
- o   help to live independently at home
- o   a "shared lives" or "adult placement" scheme – usually suitable for the needs of younger disabled adults (aged 18 to 64)

You should also consider alternatives such as "extra care" housing schemes or warden-controlled sheltered accommodation. These options offer independence with an increased level of care and support.

Personal care or nursing care?

Care homes for older people may provide personal care or nursing care. A care home registered to provide personal care will offer support, ensuring basic personal needs are taken care of. A care home providing personal care only can assist you with meals, bathing, going to the toilet and taking medication, if you need this sort of help.

Some residents may need nursing care, and some care homes are registered to provide this. These are often referred to as nursing homes. For example, a care home might specialise in certain types of disability or conditions such as dementia.

Care homes for adults aged 18 to 65

There are also residential care homes that provide care and support for younger adults with, for example, severe physical disabilities, learning disabilities, brain injury resulting from an accident, or mental health problems.

They can care for adults with more than one condition, and some homes will have expertise in providing care for adults with alcohol or drug dependency. These care homes may offer permanent residence or provide care for a temporary period.

Residential care for children and adolescents

Some care homes specialise in providing residential care for children with physical disabilities, learning disabilities or emotional problems. Residential special schools focus on education and provide teaching on-site. In some cases, care homes for children offer "transition" support for young people until they reach their early 20s.

The choice of care home to suit your needs

The law says that where the local authority is funding accommodation, it must allow a person entering residential care to choose which care home they would prefer, within reason. Social services must first agree the home is suitable for your needs and it would not cost more than you would normally pay for a home that would meet those needs.

Very importantly, local authority assistance with the cost of residential care is means-tested. You are free to make your own arrangements if you can afford the long-term cost. However, it is worth asking the local authority for a financial assessment, because it might pay some or all of your care costs.

In the financial assessment, the local authority can only take into account income and assets you own. The local authority cannot ask members of your family to pay for the basic cost of your care. If you choose a care home that costs more than the local authority usually expects to pay for a person with your needs, you may still be able to live in the care home if a relative or friend is willing and able to pay the difference between what the local authority pays and the amount the care home charges – this is known as a "top-up" fee.

However, if their situation changes and they are no longer able to pay the top-up, the local authority may have no obligation to continue to fund the more expensive care home place and you may have to move out. It is worth thinking about this potentially difficult situation when deciding on care home options.

The value of your home must not be included in the local authority's means-testing until 12 weeks after you've confirmed that the care home placement will be permanent.

It is worth now looking at the Care Act 2014, which has radically shaken up the funding of care homes, and many other areas.

The Care Act 2014

The Care Act 2014 came into force on 1st April 2015 along with a range of new supporting regulations and a single set of statutory guidance, which, taken together, describe how the Act should be applied in practice. The aim of the change is to simplify and modernise the system, which had become very complex and also to create a new approach to charging. The Care Act 2014 will actually come into force in two stages, in April 2015 and April 2016. Some of the key changes being introduced in 2015 are:

- o The promotion of individual well-being as an overarching principle within all the activities of a local authority including: assessment, eligibility, prevention, means testing and care and support planning.

- o New national eligibility criterion for both the adult requesting services and their carer(s) leading to rights to services and based around the well-being principle. The previous four local eligibility levels have now become one, set at approximately the previous 'substantial' level. Carers now have an absolute right to have their assessed, eligible, support needs met for the first time; they have a slightly different eligibility criterion to the service user, but are subject to the same means test rules.

- o A person-centred, outcomes-focused, approach to assessing and meeting needs. Local authorities must consider how to meet each person's specific needs rather than simply considering what existing service they will fit into. They must also consider what someone wants/needs to achieve or do and the effect on them of any difficulties they are having.

- The whole system is now administered via personal budgets and based on the principles of the personalisation policy that has been developed over the past few years.
- A 'right to request' service provision for a fee where someone with eligible needs is found to be a self-funder (must pay the whole cost of a service) in the means test. This right does not exist for care home provision.
- New local authority 'market shaping' duties to ensure adequate, diverse, good quality, local service provision.
- The duty to prevent, reduce and delay the need for services and also related duties to integrate care with the NHS where this benefits a service user.
- A lifetime care cost cap (£72,000 in 2016) above which the State will meet the cost of paying a person's eligible social care needs. The national cap will be reviewed every five years.
- The introduction of care accounts, which will require a local authority to track a person's personal expenditure towards meeting their eligible social care needs, towards the new care cost cap —based on the amount set out in their personal budget. Each account will be adjusted annually in line with the national rise in average earnings. Some local authorities may start to assess for care accounts ahead of the April 2016 start date to avoid capacity issues.
- An increased upper capital limit from £23,250 to £27,000 for non-residential care and support. This includes sheltered accommodation and supported living schemes, which are treated differently to care homes in the means test rules.
- An increased tariff income/lower capital limit from £14,250 to £17,000. You should be allowed to keep capital below this level.
- Independent personal budgets for those people with assessed, eligible, needs but who have capital in excess of the

upper threshold and who are meeting the cost of their care and support themselves. This is a choice that will be available to enable payments to be noted in the person's care account.

There are a wide range of support services that can be provided to help you stay in your own home and also to assist your carer if you have one. Services could include: domiciliary (home) carer and personal assistants; meals delivered at home; day centre attendance and respite care; live-in care services; rehabilitation services; sheltered accommodation and supported living; shared lives services; other housing options; community support; counselling; direct payment support organisations; information, brokerage and advice services1. Other forms of assistance could include the provision of specialist disability equipment, adaptations to your home, community alarms and other types of assistive technology.

There are certain fundamental rules that local authorities must abide by. Charges should not reduce the income that a person has left below a set level. If a person is 60 or over, this is the Pension Credit Guarantee credit level plus a buffer which is dependant where you live in the UK, for example 25% in England and 35% in Wales. The assessment should be based only on your income and generally not that of your partner or anyone else. If you feel that you are paying too much for your care services then you have the right to ask the local authority to review your financial assessment.

How the care is paid for
Either the local authority will pay you direct in cash for your services or, if you so desire, you can ask the local authority to arrange and pay for the care. The Government has also introduced a new scheme called Individual Budgets, arising out of the Care Act 2014, which are similar to Direct Payment, so you receive a cash sum, but it covers a wide range of services so it includes, for

example, help towards a warden in sheltered housing. The aim of cash payments is to put the individual in more control of the services that they buy. Obviously, this may not be suited to everyone and some people will be more reliant on the local authority to provide and pay for services.

Other benefits available

There are other benefits available such as personal independence payment (replacing Disability Living allowance for those up to age 64) or if you are over 65 Attendance Allowance. These benefits are tax-free and are not means tested. If you are a carer, you will also have the right to a free needs assessment to pay for extra levels of need.

The care plan devised by the local authority might for example recommend that someone be paid for sitting with a relative whilst you have a few hours off, or respite care (where the disabled person moves temporarily into a care home). You will be expected to pay for these services un

Important considerations when making a decision

If you do decide to enter some form of care home, there are a number of things that you can do to ensure that the care home that you have chosen is suitable for you and is well run. You should check the most recent inspection report to see how well the care home is doing and if there is anything of concern. You can get inspection reports by searching for the care home on the Care Quality Commission website or Ofsted for children's care homes. Also, consider the location of a care home, is it near family and friends, are there shops, leisure or educational facilities in the area? Other things to consider are:

- o Is the area noisy, is the care home focused on the residents' individual needs, or do they insist that residents adapt to their routine?

o What arrangements are there for visitors?
o Can residents come and go as they please, as far as it is safe to do so?
o Are staff able to help residents to go out?
o Are outings arranged? What involvement would you have in the care home?
o How would you communicate with staff?
o Are there any support groups or regular meetings?
o If safety and security are issues, what arrangements or supervision can the care home provide?
o Will the care home meet your specific religious, ethnic, cultural or social needs? Will the correct diet be provided?
o Will the right language be spoken? Will there be opportunities to participate in religious activities? Do they allow pets?

Choosing accommodation may be a lifelong decision, so you may want to think about planning for end of life care at the same time. You might also want to check what people who have used the care home say about it from online feedback and review services, such as those put together on NHS Choices. Ask for a temporary stay in the care home before you decide. Temporary stays in care homes can also be arranged in certain circumstances, such as after a stay in hospital. there are differences between good and bad care homes.

A good care home will:

o offer new residents and their families or carers a guide (in a variety of accessible formats) describing what they can expect while they're living there
o have staff who have worked there for a long time, know the residents well, and are friendly, supportive and respectful

- employ well-trained staff, particularly where specialist care such as dementia nursing is required
- involve residents, carers and their families in decision-making
- support residents in doing things for themselves and maximising their independence
- offer a choice of tasty and nutritious food, and provide a variety of leisure and social activities taking residents' needs into account
- be a clean, bright and hygienic environment that's adapted appropriately for residents, with single bedrooms available
- respect residents' privacy, modesty, dignity and choices
- be accredited under the Gold Standards Framework for end of life care

An unsatisfactory care home might:
- have a code of practice, but not adhere to it
- fail to take into account residents' needs and wishes, with most decisions made by staff
- let residents' care plans become out of date, or fail to reflect their needs accurately
- have staff who enter residents' rooms without knocking, and talk about residents within earshot of other people
- deny residents their independence – for example, by not allowing someone to feed themselves because it "takes too long"
- have staff who don't make an effort to interact with residents and leave them sitting in front of the TV all day
- be in a poorly maintained building, with rooms that all look the same and have little choice in furnishings
- need cleaning, with shared bathrooms that aren't cleaned regularly

If you move into a care home, make sure the management and staff of the home know about your condition, disability and other needs. They may have some of this information already – for example, if the local authority has set up the placement after a care needs assessment.

Moving home can be unsettling at the best of times, so when you move into a care home, it's good to have it planned in advance and have family or friends around you when you move to make you feel more comfortable. You should also:

- o contact the benefits office, if you have one (including disability benefits, as these can be affected by care home stays)
- o make sure other services at your previous address have been notified
- o let friends and family know your know contact details and when you might feel up to receiving visitors

Rights of care home residents

The Care Quality Commission (CQC) is the regulator of health and adult social care in England, whether it's provided by the NHS, local authorities, private companies or voluntary organisations.
Under existing rules, independent healthcare and adult social services must be registered with the CQC. NHS providers, such as hospitals and ambulance services, must also be registered.

The registration of organisations reassures the public when they receive a care service or treatment. It also enables the CQC to check that organisations are continuing to meet CQC standards. Standards for care homes are outlined on the CQC website. These standards are underpinned by regulations governing the quality and safety of services. The regulations are enforceable by law – the CQC can enforce fines, public warnings, or even suspend or close a service if they believe people's basic rights or safety are at risk.

Care home closures

Care homes will sometimes close. This can be because the owner decides not to carry on providing the service in that location (for instance, if they retire), or because the home has been sold or failed to meet legal standards. Proposals to close a care home can obviously cause great distress. If the care home is operated by the local authority, it has to follow a consultation process with residents and families. It may be best to get specialist legal advice in this situation. You can find an appropriate solicitor through the Law Society.

****

Chapter 6

Whilst You Are in Hospital

Information for disabled people going into hospital

If you are disabled and you need hospital treatment, it is important that you inform the hospital about the nature of your disability and the extra support you need. If your local doctor refers you for treatment, they will inform the hospital staff of your needs. You can also discuss your requirements with members of hospital staff when they complete your admission form on your arrival in hospital. The admission form gives hospital staff an idea of how much help you may need during your stay in hospital. You might want to discuss:

- o any routines you have
- o specialist equipment that the hospital may not be able to provide
- o having a carer present with you at certain times
- o access to facilities, such as bathrooms and toilets
- o using a fixed loop or subtitles for television or radio

Benefits

Before you go into hospital, it is important to notify the relevant benefit authorities. For more information about how a hospital stay will affect your benefits, see GOV.UK website on Financial help if you are disabled.

Consent to treatment

For some procedures, including operations, you will be asked to sign a consent form. For more information, see Consent to treatment.

Most people with disabilities wil be asked to give their consent to any treatment in hospitals. However, where people lack capacity to give consent, they will be treated under the Mental Capacity Act.

Where a person clearly lacks the capacity to make decisions at the time they are admitted to hospital, health professionals will make what is called a 'best interests decision' on whether specific treatment is in a person's best interests. Doctors and nurses will weigh up the benefits and risks, including whether the person is likely to regain capacity and regain the ability to give or withhold consent.

Leaving hospital

If you are disabled, staff will arrange transport for you, if necessary, to return home when you leave the hospital. If you have recently become disabled, or have given birth to a disabled child, the hospital will tell local social services so that you get the help you need.

****

Chapter 7

Disabled Children

In this chapter, we will look at the rights of the disabled child and the rights of their parents. Pregnancy and maternity is now one of the protected characteristics in the Equality Act 2010 and there is now implied into every woman's term of employment a maternity equality clause (s 73 Equality Act 2010). The Act protects women from direct discrimination (s 13(1)) and indirect discrimination (s 19(1)) in relation to pregnancy and maternity.

Right to maternity leave

All pregnant employees are entitled to 52 weeks maternity leave. This consists of 26 weeks Ordinary Maternity Leave and 26 weeks Additional Maternity Leave. This is available to all employees from the first day of employment. The employee can choose when they start their leave but the earliest it can start is 101 weeks before the baby is due. The only women not entitled to maternity leave are:

o Share fisherwomen
o Women who normally work abroad (unless they have a work connection with the UK
o Policewomen and women serving in the armed forces

Compulsory maternity leave

An employer may not permit an employee to work during her compulsory maternity period. Compulsory maternity leave is a period of two weeks commencing on the day on which childbirth occurs. An employer who allows a pregnant person to work can be fined.

Giving notice to the employer

In order to qualify for maternity leave the employer must be informed by the end of the 15th week before the baby is due:

- o   that the employee is pregnant
- o   the week in which the baby is expected; and
- o   the date when the employee intends to start ordinary maternity leave.

There is no obligation to put this in writing unless asked to. However, it is a good idea to do so. Once the employer has been informed that maternity leave will be taken they have 28 days to inform you when maternity leave starts.

If the employee has already a contractual right to maternity pay/leave, she may exercise her right to the more favourable terms. If there is a redundancy situation during the leave period and it is not practicable because of the redundancy for the employer to continue to employ her under her existing contract, she is entitled to be offered a suitable vacancy before her employment ends. If a woman intends to return to work before the end of maternity leave, 56 days notice must be given. Since women who qualify now have the right to take Additional Maternity Leave, and there is no obligation to notify the employer during the initial notification, then until notification of a return to work is given, the women will retain the right to return but not pay.

Work during the maternity leave period

Regulation 12A provides that an employee may carry out up to ten days work for her employer during her statutory maternity period (excluding the compulsory maternity period) without bringing her maternity period to an end.

Time off for Ante-natal care

To qualify for this right the employee must have made an

appointment for ante-natal care on the advice of a doctor, midwife or health visitor. The employer may not refuse time off for the first visit, but for further appointments, the employer may ask for a certificate or appointment card or other evidence.

Statutory Maternity Pay

The Social Security Act of 1996 and the Statutory Maternity Pay regulations of the same year entitle certain employees to statutory maternity pay. This has been amended by the 2002 Employment Act. SMP is paid for a maximum of 39 weeks. For the first six weeks of maternity leave SMP is paid at 90% of the average gross weekly earnings (before tax and NI) for the remaining 33 weeks it is paid at 90% of gross weekly earnings or £139.58 a week (2015-2016) whichever is the lower.

To claim SMP, a person must tell their employer, 28 days before maternity leave, that they are pregnant and will be off work because of birth. A medical certificate has to be provided.

When is SMP paid?

How long SMP is paid for depends on when the baby is due. It is paid up to 39 weeks. The earliest a person can start maternity leave and start to get SMP is 11 weeks before the baby is due. The latest date to start maternity leave and receiving SMP is the week after the week when the baby is born.

If a person is sick with a pregnancy related illness before the baby is due, SMP will start the week following the week that sickness began. If a person is sick with a non-pregnancy related illness they can claim Statutory Sick pay until the week that the baby is due.

Maternity Allowance

If an employee is not entitled to get SMP they may be entitled to maternity allowance instead. This is administered through Jobcentre

Plus and a person might get maternity benefit if:

- o   they are employed, but not eligible for SMP
- o   they are registered self-employed and paying class C National Insurance Contributions (NIC's) or hold a Small Earnings Exemption Certificate
- o   they have been very recently employed or self-employed.

Further, they may be eligible if:

- o   they have been employed or self employed for at least 26 weeks in the 'test period' (66 weeks up to and including the week before the week the baby is due) part weeks count as full weeks; and
- o   they earned £30 a week averaged over any 13 week period in the test period.

Returning to work after maternity leave

There is an automatic right to return to work after maternity leave and it is assumed the person will do so unless they state otherwise. If a person decides to return earlier than the date notified by the employer, then at least 56 days notice must be given of returning.

Parental leave

The Maternity and Parental Leave Regulations 1999 provide that every person who cares for a young child, or has recently adopted a child, can take time off from work at his or her own convenience to care for that child. Minimum provisions are set for leave, preconditions are set for leave and the notice that an employee has to give an employer before leave can be taken is set out. Employers and employees can agree to vary these provisions by using a workforce agreement as long as it is equal to or more favorable than the statutory provisions.

Any employee who has one year's continuous employment at the date the leave is due to start, and who has, or expects to have, responsibility for a child at that time can apply to take parental leave. A person will have responsibility for a child under the regulations if he/she has parental responsibility under the Children Act 1989 or is registered as the father under the provision of the Births and Deaths Register Act. The leave entitlement is up to 4 weeks unpaid parental leave per year while the child is under the age of 5, subject to an overall maximum of 18 weeks leave in respect of each child. If there are twins, each parent can take 26 weeks parental leave. The leave for the parent of a disabled child is 18 weeks per child. the leave for parents of an adopted child is 18 weeks up to their 18th birthday or 5th anniversary of their adoption, whichever comes first.

Employers can request records of leave already taken with previous employers; the entitlement is per child and not per employer. The employee can take leave in blocks of 1 week (or blocks of one day where the child is disabled) to a maximum of 4 weeks in respect of an individual child in an individual year. (Part time employees get a pro-rata entitlement.)

Paternity leave

In addition, the 2002 Employment Act widened the scope and range of paternity leave. The Act introduced the right to two weeks paid leave in addition to the 13 weeks unpaid leave. This became effective from April 2003. Leave must be taken within 8 weeks of the birth of the child or placement of the child through adoption. For employees to claim paternity leave they must:

- o Be employed and have worked for their employer for at least 26 weeks before the end of the 15th week before the expected week of childbirth; and
- o Be the biological father of the child, or be married to or be the partner of the baby's mother (this includes same sex partners, whether or not they are registered civil partners); and

o Have some responsibility for the child's upbringing; and

o Have given the employer the correct notice to take paternity leave.

o Paternity leave can be taken as a single block of either one or two weeks.

All terms and conditions of employment remain intact during the period of paternity leave except the right to remuneration. Employees are entitled to return to the jobs they had before they took paternity leave.

The Additional Paternity Leave Regulations 2010

The Additional Paternity Leave Regulations 2010 recognised that mothers can often be the main earner for the family and aims to promote shared parenting. The regulations enabled eligible employees to have the right to take additional paternity leave and pay. However the right only affected parents of children that were due to be born on or after the 3rd April 2011 or where one or both of the parents had received adoptive notification on or after the 3rd April 2011 that they have been matched with a child for adoption.

Additional Paternity Leave (APL) allowed a father to take up to 26 weeks leave to care for a child and also allowed mothers to 'transfer' up to 6 months of maternity leave to their partner. APL started 20 weeks after the birth of the child and ended no later then the child's first birthday.

However, Additional Paternity Leave is to be replaced by Shared parental leave for babies born on or after April 5th 2015. Therefore, for the purposes of this book we will refer to the new regulations outlined below.

Shared parental leave

Shared parental leave is available for babies with an expected week of childbirth (EWC) starting on or after 5 April 2015. The new right is governed by the Shared Parental Leave Regulations 2014, in force from 1 December 2014. The following deals with the main features of the draft regulations; the detail could, of course, change when the final regulations are published.

A woman, who is eligible for shared parental leavel has the right to bring her maternity leave and pay period to an end early and convert the outstanding period of maternity leave and pay into a period of shared parental leave and pay that can be taken by either parent. Shared parental leave can be taken in a more flexible way than maternity leave. It does not have to be a single continuous period; leave periods can be as little as a week and both parents can be absent from work at the same time.

Shared parental leave must be taken before the child's first birthday and is in addition to the right to unpaid parental leave under the Maternity and Parental Leave Regulations 1999. The existing right to additional paternity leave is replaced by the new right to shared parental leave, although remains in place for babies with an EWC starting before 5 April 2015.

A parent taking adoption leave also has the right to convert a period of adoption leave into a period of shared parental leave which either parent can take in a flexible way if they have a matching date on or after 5 April 2015. Below are the main points of the new regulations:

o The right to shared parental leave applies to babies with an expected week of childbirth starting on or after 5 April 2015. The default position remains that a woman is entitled to 52 weeks' maternity leave and 39 weeks' maternity pay.

o However, a woman on maternity leave can commit to bringing her maternity leave and pay period to an end early. The balance of the maternity leave and pay period becomes available for either parent to take as shared parental leave and pay.

- o Shared parental leave can be taken in periods of a week or multiples of a week at a time.
- o A parent can take a period of shared parental leave at the same time that the other parent is on maternity leave or shared parental leave
- o A parent will only qualify to take shared parental leave if the other parent meets basic work and earnings criteria and the parent taking the leave meets the individual eligibility criteria (such as having 26 weeks' continuous service at the 15th week before the EWC and remaining in the same employment).
- o An employer must have at least eight weeks' notice of any period of shared parental leave.
- o Each parent can make up to three requests for periods of shared parental leave. Whether the employer can refuse a request depends on whether the employee has asked for a continuous or discontinuous period of leave.
- o Shared parental leave has to be taken before the child's first birthday

Rights during a period of shared parental leave mirror those of a woman on maternity leave: all terms and conditions of employment continue except those relating to remuneration.

If employees suffer any detrimental treatment or are dismissed as a result of taking or asking to take shared parental leave they can bring a complaint to the employment tribunal.

Adoption leave and pay

The 2002 Employment Act creates a right for parents to take adoption leave when permanently adopting a child. An adoptive parent is entitled to take 26 weeks paid adoption leave (known as 'ordinary adoption leave') and up to 26 weeks unpaid adoption leave During ordinary adoption leave, employees will be entitled to receive Statutory Adoption Pay (SAP) for 39 weeks of £139.58 per week (2015-2016) or 90% of earnings, whichever is the lower. You should check with the DTI or DSS for current rates.

Qualifying requirements

To be entitled to take adoption leave, employees must have attained 26 weeks service with their employer at the date the adoption takes place. Leave can be taken at any time after the adoption placement begins. Employees will be required to provide evidence of the adoption to the employer. Only one partner in a couple will be able to take adoption leave. The other partner, male or female, will be able to take paternity leave for 2 weeks and receive SPP. There are statutory notice provisions covering how and when employees must inform employers that they wish to take adoption leave. These are flexible and can be verified with the employer.

During the period of ordinary adoption leave the employee is entitled to all their terms and conditions, except the right to remuneration. During the period of additional adoption leave, the employee is in the same position as someone on additional maternity leave – namely that whilst most of the terms and conditions of employment will be suspended, those relating to notice, confidentiality, implied terms of mutual trust and confidence, redundancy terms and disciplinary and grievance procedures will remain in place. The right to return after either ordinary or additional adoption leave mirror's the provisions for ordinary and additional maternity leave respectively.

Disabled children's benefits

We have described the range of benefits available to those who are disabled or care for disabled people, in Chapter 2. However, there is specific help for disabled children as outlined below.

From birth, you should register your child with the local authority social care department. You can also apply to the authority for an assessment of your child's special needs. If your child is registered as blind you can apply for

- o A disabled child premium in the assessment of your housing benefit and health benefits and a disabled child element with your tax credit. If you are claiming universal credit, the higher rate of the disabled child addition will be included in your calculation.
- o You can also get a 50% reduction in your TV licence if you transfer the licence into the child's name.

If you want any more details about benefits and rights you should contact the Royal National Institute for the Blind on 0303 123 9999 www.rnib.org.uk.

Additional help-Family Fund

You can get help from the Family Fund with some of the additional costs arising from the child's disability. the purpose of this fund is to help families with the day-to-day care of a severely disabled child through the provision of grants and information concerning care. the Family Fund is an independent charity and is financed by the government.

You can receive help from the fund if you are providing care at home for a severely disabled child under the age of 18 and are entitled to tax credits and certain other benefits. You cannot get help for a child in Local Authority care.

The help that the Family Fund can provide is:

- o Holidays or leisure activities for the whole family
- o Washing machine and dryer for extra washing arising from caring for a child
- o Bedding and clothing if there is additional wear and tear.

o IT equipment
o Play equipment related to your child's special needs.

The first step is to contact the Family Fund by phone or online as follows:

Tel: 0844 974 4099
Online www.familyfund.org.uk

Usually the first step after contact is to receive a visit from a representative of the Fund.

Loans and grants to assist in the care of a disabled child
If you have been receiving Income Support, Income Related Employment and Support Allowance, Income Based Job Seekers Allowance or Pension Credit for at least 26 weeks you may be eligible for a budgeting loan to help meet one off costs. You need to contact your local authority to obtain more details.

Home adaptations
As outlined in Chapter 8 you may be eligible for adaptations in the home, including a Disabled Facilities Grant You should contact your local authority for more information.

Healthy Start Vouchers
The Healthy Start Scheme provides vouchers for fresh milk, infant formula milk and fresh or frozen fruit and vegetables. It also provides coupons to claim free vitamin supplements without a prescription. There are certain criteria for eligibility:

o You must be at least ten weeks pregnant and under 18 and not subject to immigration control o You are at least ten weeks pregnant or have a child under 4 and you or a member of your family receive income-related employment and support allowance , income support, income based job seekers allowance or child tax credit and your income is below £16,190. You can get more information about Healthy Start on the Healthy Start Helpline 0845 607 6823 or from the website www.healthystart.nhs.uk

There may be help also through the Nursery Milk Scheme, which is available for children under 5 who attend approved day care facilities for two or more hours a day and also some 4 year olds in reception classes. For more information go to www.nurserymilk.co.uk.

Disability Living Allowance-Care Component

We discussed DLA in chapter 2, benefits. However, for a child you can be paid care component when they reach three months of age. there are situations when you can claim beforehand. If your baby is terminally ill they will automatically qualify for the highest rate of DLA as soon as you claim DLA after birth. If your baby is awarded DLA you may get a disabled child premium included in the assessment of housing and health benefits and also in the assessment of your child tax credit (see below) or in the assessment of Universal Credit. Other benefits may be enhanced. Contact your local Jobcentre Plus for details.

As the child develops the following will apply:

o From 2 years of age you can claim Vaccine damage payment. This scheme provides a tax-free lump sum for someone who is, or was immediately before death severely disabled as a result of vaccination against specific diseases. For full details of the scheme including definitions you should contact: the Vaccine Damage Payments Unit, Palatine House, Lancaster House, Preston, Lancs PR1 1HB. Tel: 01772 899 944 or go to www.gov.uk/vaccine-damage-payment.

o   Your child will be eligible for a Special Educational Needs Assessment-Local Authorities in England and Wales have a duty to identify any child who might have special educational needs. You should contact your local authority for details.

o   You may also be able to apply for a Blue badge parking concession (see chapter on transport) once the child reaches 2 years of age. You can also apply for a child under 2 if there is a need to transport bulky equipment arising from the child's disability.

o   As mentioned above, from 3 years of age, you can apply for the higher rate of DLA.

o   From 5 years of age the child can be awarded a DLA lower rate component.

o   From 5 years of age the child will be eligible for free school meals, dependant on the benefits you receive and savings. School clothing grants and travel concessions may also be available.

o   From 8 years of age, if your child has to travel more than 3 miles to school they can receive help. For a disabled child you may get help even if the distance is less than 3 miles.

o   From the age of 16 years old a disabled child has the option of claiming for benefits in their own rights.

o   Other help is available, as outlined in Chapter 2, such as carer's allowance, low income benefits, housing benefits, council tax support and help with mortgage and interest costs. there is also help with home adaptations (outlined in chapter) help with child support and help from the family fund.

Eligibility for child benefit

All people can get child benefit if they have responsibility for a dependant child (under 16) or a qualifying young person (under 20 and in full time non-advanced education-more than 12 hours a week at school or college or approved education which is non-waged)). You have to pass the residence test and not be subject to immigration control. You do not have to be the parent or stay-at-home guardian.

You won't be eligible for child benefit if the child or young person is in local authority care or in detention for more than 8 weeks, although their are exceptions to this. You will not be eligible if you are a foster parent and get an allowance to look after the child or prospective adopter of a child placed with you by a local authority. In addition, if the young person is married, in a civil partnership or cohabiting you won't be eligible. However, special rules will apply if the child if the child is in residential accommodation provided for them because of their disability.

Guardians allowance

This is a tax free benefit for someone who is looking after someone who is effectively an orphan. You can get guardians allowance for someone who is not your birth child or adopted child and both parents of the child are dead, or one is dead and the other is missing, divorced or had their civil partnership dissolved and liable for neither maintenance or custody of the child, serving a prison sentence of more than 2 years from the date that the other parent dies or detained in hospital under sections of the Mental Health Act 1983 or other associated legislation.

The current rates of child benefit and guardians allowance

The current rates of child benefit (2015/16) are:

Only/eldest child or qualifying young person-£20.70 per week

Subsequent children £13.70

Guardians allowance-£16.55 per week.

For more information on child benefit and how to claim you should contact the Child Benefit helpline on 0300 200 3100: textphone 0300 200 3103 (there are other rules governing the payment of child benefit. Child benefit is administered by HMRC and full details of the rules governing payment and eligibility can be obtained from them via their website hmrc.gov.uk).

****

Chapter 8

Disabled People and Employment

We have already seen that there are a range of benefits available for disabled people who are either out of work or who wish to re-enter the workplace. This chapter covers the support and training available to help disabled people back into work. It also covers employers responsibilities towards disabled people in the workplace.

Entering employment

The role of Jobcentre plus and Disability Employment Advisors

Jobcentre plus is the Department of Work and Pensions organisation providing benefits and services to people of working age. This means age 16 or over. Everyone who claims benefits from Jobcentre Plus is allocated a personal advisor to deal with claims for benefit and help them back into work. Disabled people also have access to a Disability Employment Advisor who provide employment assessment, job seeking advice and assistance with training as well as specialist advice and information. It is important to note that advice and support from a DEA is not dependant on benefits it is available to any disabled person.

Work programmes

There are a number of work programmes managed by 'providers' who are contracted by the government which aim to help people find work and stay in work. They provide activities such as work experience, work trials, help to become self-employed, voluntary work, training and ongoing support. The programmes are mandatory if you are considered capable of work. Referral to work programmes is normally through Jobcentre Plus. If you are in receipt of Job Seekers Allowance you will have to take part in the Work Programme after nine months. If your advisor agrees you may join earlier than this if you wish. If you receive Employment and Support Allowance the time for entry to a Work Programme will vary depending on an assessment of your fitness to work.

Community Work Placement Programme

The Community Work Placement Programme is designed for Jobseeker's Allowance claimants who require further support to obtain and sustain employment following a Work Programme placement. Participants may have to undertake work placements for the benefit of the community and work-related activity. This programme is mandatory.

Work Choice

the work choice programme is aimed at people who are experiencing barriers to work arising from a disability or who are in work but risk losing their job as a result of a disability. Participation is voluntary and usually you must be referred by a Disability Employment Advisor. Work choice consists of three modules, each of which is tailored to your specific needs:

o Work Entry Support-this is up to six months help with vocational guidance, confidence building, job search advice and other support such as job application skills. In some cases, this support can be for longer than six months;

o In-Work Support-this is up to two years support once you are in employment. The Work Choice Provider will work with you and your employer to identify the support needed and also help you develop the necessary skills and knowledge to move to unsupported employment;

o Longer Term In-Work Support- This is long term support offered to assist you throughout your career.

Work choice is available throughout the UK with the exception of Northern Ireland where there are similar schemes.

Access to Work

Access to Work is designed to help disabled people overcome any barriers that they may face in obtaining employment and retaining employment. Access to Work provides practical advice and also grants towards extra costs which may be incurred arising from a disability. This advice and support can include special aids and adaptations, or equipment needed for employment, adaptations premises (not new) and equipment, help with travel, help with a support worker, a communicator and, if needed, an interpreter.

Certain types of expenditure are excluded, details of which can be obtained during the application stage. Costs which are the responsibility of the employer, for example costs which are seen as a 'reasonable adjustment' under the Equality Act 2010, are not included. (See below for details of 'reasonable adjustments').

You will be eligible for help through the Access to Work scheme if you are employed, including as an apprentice, self-employed or unemployed and have a job to start and you are disabled. Access to Work defines disability as in the Equality Act 2010 (see introduction) but also includes impairments and health conditions that are only evident in the workplace.

Access to Work also provides help to people with mental health conditions and learning difficulties. The service provides a wide range of support for a period of six months for people with mental health conditions, including work focussed mental health support tailored to the individual, assessment of an individuals needs, a personalised support plan, advice and guidance to employers and the identification of reasonable adjustments needed in the workplace.

How much support can you receive?

If you have been in a job for less than six weeks, are self-employed or are about to start work, Access to Work will cover 100% of approved costs. If you have been employed for six weeks or more when you apply for help, Access to Work will pay only some of the costs of support, called 'cost sharing' which is dependant on the number of employees in an organisation. The funding agreements can last up to three years with an annual review.

For more information about Access to Work contact 020 8426 3110. Normally there will be a telephone interview by an advisor to assess your eligibility. Following the phone interview you should be sent an application form (AtW1), which you should check, sign and return within a given period.

Training

There are numerous government training programmes designed to help prepare people for work. You can find details from your nearest Jobcentre Plus office. There are many courses available designed to help disabled people. You should contact a disabled employment advisor at the local Jobcentre Plus office or you can ring the National Careers Service Helpline 0800 100 900 or Skills Development Scotland 0800 917 8000.

Benefits while training

DLA and PIP are not usually affected if you undertake training or if you get a training allowance. However, DLA care component and PIP daily living component will not usually be paid for any days that you stay in a care home to attend a residential training programme. The residential training programmes aim to help long-term unemployed adults overcome disability related barriers to employment.

Advice concerning your benefits entitlement, such as Income Support, Jobseeker's allowance and Employment and Support Allowance and how they are affected by training, can be obtained from your local Jobcentre Plus.

When you are In Work

Disability and employers responsibilities

It's against the law for employers to discriminate against you because of a disability. The Equality Act 2010 protects you and covers areas including:

- o   application forms
- o   interview arrangements
- o   aptitude or proficiency tests
- o   job offers
- o   terms of employment, including pay
- o   promotion, transfer and training opportunities
- o   dismissal or redundancy
- o   discipline and grievances

Reasonable adjustments in the workplace

Those employees with disabilities share the same employment rights as other workers with the addition of some other rights as stated within the Equality Act 2010. Within this act, employers are expected to make 'reasonable adjustments' within the workplace with regard to access and facilities for disabled members of staff. The provisions set out in the Equality Act apply to every employer, no matter the size or industry (except the armed forces). It is worth noting that the reasonable adjustment requirements are not necessary to carry out in anticipation or only in case an employer gains a disabled employee. The adjustments need only be carried out once a disabled person is employed or applies for a role within the company.

To comply with the Equality Act 2010, an employee must suffer from severe or long-term impairments. Impairments of disabled employees include:

o   Physical impairments - mobility disabilities
o   Mental impairments - long term (12 months plus) mental illnesses or learning disabilities
o   Sensory impairments - visual or hearing impairments.

What are reasonable adjustments?

The Equality Act states employers have a duty to amend the workplace in order to accommodate both disabled employees and/or applicants for job roles. These adjustments are in order to avoid disabled people being at a disadvantage when applying for a job or indeed working within an organisation. Reasonable adjustments can vary and cover areas from working arrangements to physical changes around the workplace.

Adjusted working arrangements may be flexible working hours to allow disabled employees to be able to meet their employment requirements, or amendments being made to workplace equipment, adapting it to suit employee's capabilities.

If a physical feature within the workplace creates a disadvantage for a disabled employee, steps must be taken to amend or remove the obstruction. Physical adjustments can include changes such as:

o   The addition of a ramp rather than steps to access buildings.
o   Providing disabled toilet facilities need to provided to accommodate those that need them.
o   The widening of doorways to allow for wheelchair access.

o Repositioning door handles and/or light switches etc to ensure they can be reached.

In some cases, an employer may need to provide disabled employees with extra help through an aid to ensure that the disabled employee is not at any disadvantage against other workers. This aid may be in form of specialist or adapted equipment, such as special computer keyboards or telephones.

With regard to a disabled person applying for a job, an employer does not necessarily need to make the physical adjustments before the interview. It will suffice that an easily accessible location and necessary support and assistance for the applicant to get there is provided. If the applicant is then employed, the employer must consider the other adjustments mentioned above.

Recruitment

An employer who is recruiting staff may make limited enquiries about your health or disability. You can only be asked about your health or disability:

o to help decide if you can carry out a task that is an essential part of the work
o to help find out if you can take part in an interview
o to help decide if the interviewers need to make reasonable adjustments for you in a selection process
o to help monitoring
o if they want to increase the number of disabled people they employ
o if they need to know for the purposes of national security checks

You may be asked whether you have a health condition or disability on an application form or in an interview. You need to think about whether the question is one that is allowed to be asked at that stage of recruitment.

Redundancy and retirement

You can't be chosen for redundancy just because you're disabled. The selection process for redundancy must be fair and balanced for all employees. Also, your employer cannot force you to retire if you become disabled.

Claiming benefits as a result of a work-related disability
Industrial Injuries disablement benefit

You might get Industrial Injuries Disablement Benefit (IIDB) if you're ill or disabled from an accident or disease caused by work while you were on an approved employment training scheme or course. The amount you may get depends on your individual circumstances. Your carer could get Carer's Allowance if you have substantial caring needs.

What you'll get

The level of your disability will affect the amount of benefit you may get. This will be assessed by a 'medical advisor' on a scale of 1 to 100%. Normally you must be assessed as 14% disabled or more to get the benefit. The amounts outlined below are a guide only.

Assessed level of disablement	Weekly amount
100%	£168.00
90%	£151.20
80%	£134.40
70%	£117.60

Assessed level of disablement	Weekly amount
60%	£100.80
50%	£84.00
40%	£67.20
30%	£50.40
20%	£33.60

Eligibility
Accidents

You may be able to claim Industrial Injuries Disablement Benefit if:

- o   you were employed when the accident or event happened
- o   you were on an approved employment training scheme or course when the accident or event happened
- o   the work accident or event that caused your illness or disability happened in England, Scotland or Wales.

Diseases

You can claim IIDB if you were employed in a job or were on an approved employment training scheme or course that caused your disease. The scheme covers a number of diseases including:

- o   asthma
- o   chronic bronchitis or emphysema
- o   deafness
- o   pneumoconiosis (including silicosis and asbestosis)
- o   osteoarthritis of the knee in coal miners
- o   prescribed disease A11 (previously known as vibration white finger)
- o   diffuse mesothelioma and a number of other asbestos-related diseases such as primary carcinoma of the lung

The scheme also covers asbestos related diseases including:

- pneumoconiosis (asbestosis)
- diffuse mesothelioma
- primary carcinoma of the lung with asbestosis
- primary carcinoma of the lung without asbestosis but where there has been extensive occupational exposure to asbestos in specified occupations
- unilateral or bilateral diffuse pleural thickening.
- You can get a full list of illnesses from your regional Industrial Injuries Disablement Benefit centre.

You can't claim Industrial Injuries Disablement Benefit if you were self-employed.

Claiming for Accidents
Print and fill in form BI100A to claim Industrial Injuries Disablement Benefit (IIDB) for accidents.

Diseases
Print and fill in form BI100PD to claim IIDB for diseases. To request a form contact:

Barnsley Industrial Injuries Disablement Benefit centre
Telephone: 0345 758 5433

Send your form to Barrow Industrial Injuries Disablement Benefit Centre if you're claiming under special provisions.

Barrow Benefit Centre
Post Handling Site B
Wolverhampton
WV99 1RX

Telephone: 0345 603 1358

Textphone: 0345 608 8551

For all other claims send your form to Barnsley Industrial Injuries Disablement Benefit centre.

Barnsley IIDB Centre

Mail Handling Site A

Wolverhampton

WV98 1SY

Telephone: 0345 758 5433

Textphone: 0345 608 8551

Other benefits you may be able to get
Constant Attendance Allowance (CAA)

You can claim CAA for accidents where your disability is assessed at 100% and you need daily care and attention. The CAA rate you're paid is based on an assessment of your needs.

Exceptionally Severe Disablement Allowance

You can claim £67.20 paid in addition to the CAA rates, if you're assessed at one of the top two rates of CAA and need permanent, constant care and attention.

Reduced Earnings Allowance (REA)

You may get REA if:

o   you can't do your usual job or other work with similar pay because of an accident or disease caused by work

o   you have a disability or injury which began before 1 October 1990

o   Pneumoconiosis Etc. (Workers' Compensation) Act 1979

Jobcentre Plus may pay you a lump sum if you have one of the following diseases:

- o pneumoconiosis
- o byssinosis
- o diffuse mesothelioma
- o bilateral diffuse pleural thickening
- o primary carcinoma of the lung when accompanied by asbestosis or bilateral diffuse pleural thickening

To get a payment you must meet all the following conditions:

- o your dust-related disease must have been caused by your employment
- o you're getting Industrial Injuries Disablement Benefit for one of the listed diseases
- o you must claim within 12 months of the decision awarding Industrial Injuries Disablement Benefit
- o you can't or haven't taken civil action because your former employer has stopped trading
- o you haven't brought a court action or received compensation from an employer in respect of the disease

You may be able to make a claim if you're the dependant of someone who suffered from a dust-related disease but who has died. A dependant claim must be made within 12 months of the death of the sufferer.

Diffuse mesothelioma payment

The scheme covers people whose exposure to asbestos occurred in the United Kingdom and are not entitled to a payment under the Pneumoconiosis etc (Workers' Compensation) Act 1979. For example:

- o they came into contact with asbestos from a relative, eg by washing their clothes o their exposure to asbestos was while self-employed

You may be able to claim a one-off lump sum payment if you:

o are unable to make a claim under the 1979 Pneumoconiosis Act

o haven't received payment in respect of the disease from an employer, a civil claim or elsewhere

o aren't entitled to compensation from a Ministry of Defence scheme

Effects on other benefits

You can still get Industrial Injuries Disablement Benefit (IIDB) if you're claiming:

contribution-based Employment and Support Allowance

o Incapacity Benefit

o contribution-based Jobseeker's Allowance

o State Pension

IIDB will affect the following benefits if you or your partner are claiming them:

o Income Support

o income-based Jobseeker's Allowance

o income-related Employment and Support Allowance

o Pension Credit

o Housing Benefit

o Working Tax Credit

o Universal credit

You should also check to see if Council tax Support has been affected.

****

Chapter 9

Disabled People and Education

Education

It's against the law for a school or other education provider to treat disabled students unfavourably. This includes: direct discrimination', eg refusing admission to a student because of disability; 'indirect discrimination', eg only providing application forms in one format that may not be accessible; 'discrimination arising from a disability', eg a disabled pupil is prevented from going outside at break time because it takes too long to get there; 'harassment', eg a teacher shouts at a disabled student for not paying attention when the student's disability stops them from easily concentrating and victimisation, eg suspending a disabled student because they've complained about harassment.

Reasonable adjustments

As with employers, an education provider has a duty to make 'reasonable adjustments' to make sure disabled students are not discriminated against. These changes could include changes to physical features, eg creating a ramp so that students can enter a classroom,providing extra support and aids (like specialist teachers or equipment)

Special Educational Needs (SEN)

All publicly-funded pre-schools, nurseries, state schools and local authorities must try to identify and help assess children with Special Educational Needs. If a child has a statement of special educational needs, they should have a 'transition plan' drawn up in Year 9. This helps to plan what support the child will have after leaving school.

Higher education

All universities and higher education colleges should have a person in charge of disability issues that you can talk to about the support they offer. You can also ask local social services for an assessment to help with your day-to-day living needs.

Children with special educational needs (SEN)

Special educational needs (SEN) that affect a child's ability to learn can include their:

- o behaviour or ability to socialise, eg not being able to make friends, reading and writing, eg they have dyslexia, ability to understand things, concentration levels, eg they have Attention Deficit Hyperactivity Disorder, physical needs or impairments

If you think your child may have special educational needs, contact the 'SEN co-ordinator', or 'SENCO' in your child's school or nursery. Contact your local council if your child isn't in a school or nursery. Your local Information, Advice and Support (IAS) Service can give you advice about SEN.

Support a child can receive

A child may be eligible for SEN support - support given in school, eg speech therapy, an education, health and care plan (EHC) - a plan of care for children and young people aged up to 25 who have more complex needs. If you or your child got support before September 2014 this will continue until your local council changes to SEN support or an EHC plan.

Special educational needs support

Your child will get special educational needs (SEN) support at their school or college.

Your child may need an EHC plan if they need more support than their school provides.

Children under 5
SEN support for children under 5 includes:

- o   a written progress check when your child is 2 years old
- o   a child health visitor carrying out a health check for your child if they're aged 2 to 3
- o   a written assessment in the summer term of your child's first year of primary school
- o   making reasonable adjustments for disabled children, eg providing aids like tactile signs

Nurseries, playgroups and childminders registered with Ofsted follow the Early Years Foundation Stage (EYFS) framework. The framework makes sure that there is support in place for children with SEN.

Children between 5 and 15

Talk to the teacher or the SEN coordinator (SENCO) if you think your child needs:

- o   a special learning programme
- o   extra help from a teacher or assistant
- o   to work in a smaller group
- o   observation in class or at break
- o   help taking part in class activities
- o   extra encouragement in their learning, eg to ask questions or to try something they find difficult
- o   help communicating with other children
- o   support with physical or personal care difficulties, eg eating, getting around school safely or using the toilet

Young people aged 16 or over in further education

Contact the college or academy before your child starts further education to make sure that they can meet your child's needs. The college and your local authority will talk to your child about the support they need.

Independent support for children of all ages

Independent supporters can help you and your child through the new SEN assessment process, including:

- o replacing a statement of special educational needs with a new education, health and care plan (EHCP)
- o moving a child from a learning difficulty assessment (LDA) to EHCP

Extra help

An education, health and care (EHC) plan is for children and young people aged up to 25 who need more support than is available through special educational needs support. EHC plans identify educational, health and social needs and set out the additional support to meet those needs.

Requesting an EHC assessment

You can ask your local authority to carry out an assessment if you think your child needs an EHC plan. A request can also be made by anyone at your child's school, a doctor, a health visitor or a nursery worker. A local authority has 6 weeks to decide whether or not to carry out an EHC assessment. If they decide to carry out an assessment you may be asked for any reports from your child's school, nursery or childminder, doctors' assessments of your child, a letter from you about your child's needs.

You'll usually find out within 16 weeks whether or not an EHC plan is going to be made for your child.

Creating an EHC plan

Your local authority will create a draft EHC plan and send you a copy. You have 15 days to comment, including if you want to ask that your child goes to a specialist needs school or specialist college. Your local authority has 20 weeks from the date of the assessment to give you the final EHC plan.

Disagreeing with a decision

You can challenge your local authority about their decision to not carry out an assessment, their decision to not create an EHC plan, the special educational support in the EHC plan, the school named in the EHC plan. If you can't resolve the problem with your local authority, you can appeal to the special educational needs and disability tribunal.

Personal budgets

You may be able to get a personal budget for your child if they have an education, health and care (EHC) plan or have been told that they need an EHC plan. It allows you to have a say in how to spend the money on support for your child. There are 3 ways you can use your personal budget. You can have:

○ direct payments made into your account - you buy and manage services yourself

○ an arrangement with your local authority or school where they hold the money for you but you still decide how to spend it (sometimes called 'notional arrangements')

○ third-party arrangements - you choose someone else to manage the money for you

You can have a combination of all 3 options

If your child got support before September 2014

Your child will continue to get support until they're moved across to special educational needs (SEN) support or an education, health and care (EHC) plan.

Your child should move to:

- o SEN Support by summer 2015 if they already get help through School Action, School Action Plus, Early Years Action or Early Years Action Plus
- o an EHC plan by spring 2018 if they have a statement
- o an EHC plan by September 2016 if they have an LDA

Your school will tell you when they plan to move your child to SEN support and your council will tell you when they are going to transfer your child to an EHC plan.

Early Years Action and School Action

This support is either a different way of teaching certain things, or some help from an extra adult.

Early Years Action Plus and School Action Plus

This is extra help from an external specialist, eg a speech therapist.

Assessments

An assessment of special educational needs involves experts and people involved in your child's education. They ask about your child's needs and what should be done to meet them.

Statement

A statement of special education needs describes your child's needs and how they should be met, including what school they should go to.

Further education

If your child has a statement of special educational needs, they'll have a 'transition plan' drawn up in Year 9. This helps to plan for their future after leaving school.

Help and advice

You can call the Contact a Family helpline for help and advice.

Contact a Family helpline

helpline@cafamily.org.uk
Telephone: 0808 808 3555
Monday to Friday, 9:30am to 5pm

You can also get help from Independent Parental Special Education Advice (IPSEA).

IPSEA advice line

Telephone: 0800 018 4016
Monday to Thursday, 10am to 4pm and 7pm to 9pm
Friday, 1pm to 4pm

Disabled people and financing studies

Financial support for all students comes in the form of tuition fee loans, means tested loans for living expenses and also a range of supplementary grants and loans depending on individual circumstances. Entitlement to student support depends on where you are living and where you intend to study. For details of loan entitlement and rates also Bursaries, you should contact:

Student finance England if you reside in England-0845 300 5090
www.gov.uk/student-finance

Northern Ireland Student finance NI 0845 600 0662
www.studentfinanceni.co.uk

Scotland Student Awards Agency for Scotland 0300 555 0505
www.saas.gov.uk

Wales Student Finance Wales 0845 602 8845
www.studentfianncewales.co.uk

For details of loans and bursaries plus other sources of finance, you should contact the student support officer responsible for advice at the educational institution that you are to attend.

Students and means tested benefits

If you are a disabled student and want more information on benefits entitlement and how being a student in higher education affects benefits then you should contact the Disability Advisor at your local Jobcentre Plus. Essentially, benefit entitlement will depend very much on your individual circumstances and what type of education you are undertaking.

****

Chapter 10

Disabled People and Housing Rights

This chapter covers the rights of disabled people and occupation of a property. In the main, it deals with the responsibilities of private landlords and with the responsibilities of tenants. We also discuss accessing finance to purchase a property and the provision of disabled facilities grants to help the process of living in a property that much easier.

For more information about renting in the public sector, i.e. local authority or housing association property you should go to your local Citizens Advice Bureau or visit their website at www.citizensadvice.org.uk.

The law generally relating to tenants rights covers all people but there are also separate rights protecting those with disabilities.

Discrimination and property

The law applying to disability discrimination applies to landlords through the Equality Act 2010. Landlords have to be aware of their legal duties regarding disabled people who may need their homes to be altered or have some form of assistance to live in the homes that they are renting.

Adapting Property

Although there are certain obligations on a landlord to make adaptations, the measures that they may need to take don't include removing or altering what's defined as a physical feature of the property. A physical feature could be:

o   any feature that forms part of the way that the property is designed or constructed

o   any feature that's part of the approach to, exit from or access to the property

o   any fixtures in or on the property.

Things that a landlord would not have to do, for example, include moving a drying area or a communal entrance for a block of flats.

If a tenant asks to make adaptations, they have to make a request in writing, and any request must be 'reasonable'. It's also not necessarily up to the landlord to foot the bill for any alterations to a property that need to be carried out.

Auxiliary Aids

If a landlord rents their property to a disabled tenant, they have a duty to provide them with what's called 'auxiliary aids and services' to make it easier for them to live in the property. These only need to be provided if without them it would difficult or impossible for the tenant to enjoy full use of the property. Some things that a landlord could reasonably be expected to do are:

o   making changes to furniture and furnishings in the property

o   replacing or providing signs

o   replacing taps or door handles that are difficult for a disabled person to use

o   adapting door bells or door entry systems

Ways of Discriminating Against Disabled Tenants

There are several ways that a tenant or potential tenant can claim that a landlord has discriminated against them. They can't refuse to let the property to someone who is disabled and even if they think the property is suitable for them, still can't use that as a reason to refuse then a tenancy.

A landlord must not refuse to allow a disabled tenant the use of any communal facilities on the grounds of their disability, refuse to carry out repairs or renovations, or give them less favourable treatment in any way.

Changing The Terms of a Lease

In some cases, there may be terms in a standard tenancy agreement which make it difficult for a disabled person to live in the property. One example of this could be a ban on pets in the property, which would mean that a tenant who has, or develops, sight problems could be unable to have a sight assistance dog. In this case, it would be unreasonable to insist on this term of the tenancy agreement, and most landlords would simply waive it to allow a guide dog.

Your rights and responsibilities as a tenant

Once you have accessed a property, you will have certain rights and responsibilities. As a tenant, you have the right to:

- o   live in a property that's safe and in a good state of repair
- o   have your deposit returned when the tenancy ends - and in some circumstances have it protected
- o   challenge excessively high charges
- o   know who your landlord is
- o   live in the property undisturbed
- o   see an Energy Performance Certificate for the property
- o   be protected from unfair eviction and unfair rent
- o   have a written agreement if you have a fixed-term tenancy of more than 3 years

If you have a tenancy agreement, it should be fair and comply with the law. If you don't know who your landlord is, write to the person or company you pay rent to. Your landlord can be fined If they don't give you this information within 21 days.

In Scotland, your landlord must give you a tenant information pack when you start a new assured or short assured tenancy.

Your responsibilities

You must give your landlord access to the property to inspect it or carry out repairs. Your landlord has to give you at least 24 hours' notice and visit at a reasonable time of day, unless it's an emergency and they need immediate access. You must also:

- take good care of the property
- pay the agreed rent, even if repairs are needed or you're in dispute with your landlord
- pay other charges as agreed with the landlord, eg Council Tax or utility bills
- repair or pay for any damage caused by you, your family or friends
- only sublet a property if the tenancy agreement or your landlord allows it

Your landlord has the right to take legal action to evict you if you don't meet your responsibilities.

If your landlord lives outside the UK

Contact HM Revenue and Customs (HMRC) if your landlord lives outside the UK and you pay £100 or more a week in rent directly to them. You may have to deduct tax from your rent under HMRC's 'non-resident landlord scheme'.

Your landlord's safety responsibilities

Your landlord must keep the property you live in safe and free from health hazards.

Gas safety

Your landlord must:

- make sure gas equipment they supply is safely installed and maintained by a Gas Safe registered engineer
- have a registered engineer do an annual gas safety on each appliance and flue
- give you a copy of the gas safety check record before you move in, or within 28 days of the check
- Electrical safety

Your landlord must make sure:

- the electrical system is safe, eg sockets and light fittings
- all appliances they supply are safe, eg cookers and kettles

Fire safety

Your landlord must:

- follow fire safety regulations, eg check you have access to escape routes at all times
- make sure the furniture and furnishings they supply are fire safe
- provide fire alarms and extinguishers (if the property is a large House in Multiple Occupation (HMO)

Repairs-What your landlord must do

Your landlord is responsible for repairs to:

- the property's structure and exterior
- basins, sinks, baths and other sanitary fittings including pipes and drains
- heating and hot water
- gas appliances, pipes, flues and ventilation

o electrical wiring

o any damage they cause by attempting repairs

Your landlord is usually responsible for repairing common areas, eg staircases in blocks of flats. Check your tenancy agreement if you're unsure.

Your responsibilities

You should only carry out repairs if the tenancy agreement says you can. You can't be forced to do repairs that are your landlord's responsibility. If you damage another tenant's flat, eg if water leaks into another flat from an overflowing bath, you're responsible for paying for the repairs. You're also responsible for paying to put right any damage caused by your family and friends.

If your property needs repairs

Contact your landlord if you think repairs are needed. Do this straight away for faults that could damage health, eg faulty electrical wiring. Your landlord should tell you when you can expect the repairs to be done. You should carry on paying rent while you're waiting. If repairs are nor carried out contact the environmental health department at your local council for help. They must take action if they think the problems could harm you or cause a nuisance to others. Contact the Private Rented Housing Panel (PRHP) if you're in Scotland.

If your house isn't fit to live in

If you think your home's unsafe, contact housing department at your local council. They'll do a Housing Health and Safety Rating System (HHSRS) assessment and must take action if they think your home has serious health and safety hazards. There are different housing standards and procedures in Scotland and Northern Ireland.

Rent increases

Your tenancy agreement should include how and when the rent will be reviewed. There are special rules for increasing protected (sometimes known as 'regulated') tenancy rents.

For a periodic tenancy (rolling on a week-by-week or month-by-month basis) your landlord can't normally increase the rent more than once a year without your agreement. For a fixed-term tenancy (running for a set period) your landlord can only increase the rent if you agree. If you don't agree, the rent can only be increased when the fixed term ends.

General rules around rent increases

For any tenancy:

- o your landlord must get your permission if they want to increase the rent by more than previously agreed
- o the rent increase must be fair and realistic (ie in line with average local rents)

If the tenancy agreement lays down a procedure for increasing rent, your landlord must stick to this. Otherwise, your landlord can:

- o renew your tenancy agreement at the end of the fixed term, but with an increased rent
- o agree a rent increase with you and produce a written record of the agreement that you both sign
- o use a 'Landlord's notice proposing a new rent' form, which increases the rent after the fixed term has ended

Your landlord must give you a minimum of one month's notice (if you pay rent weekly or monthly). If you have a yearly tenancy, they must give you 6 months' notice.

Rent disputes

You can apply to a tribunal to decide on certain rent disputes in England. There are different ways to solve rent disputes in Scotland Wales and Northern Ireland. You can only apply to the tribunal if:

- o   you have an assured or assured shorthold tenancy
- o   your rent's been increased as part of a 'section 13 procedure' - the letter from your landlord will say if it has, and will tell you more about applying to the tribunal
- o   You must apply before the new rent is due to start.

New rental terms

You can ask the tribunal to decide new rental terms when you renew your tenancy.

Rent arrears

Your landlord can evict you if you fall behind with your rent - you could lose your home. You can get advice if you're in rent arrears or having difficulty in paying your rent from:
- o   Money Advice Service
- o   Shelter
- o   Citizens Advice

Deposit protection

Your landlord must put your deposit in a government-approved tenancy deposit protection scheme if you have an assured shorthold tenancy (AST) that started after 6 April 2007 (in England and Wales).

Deposit disputes

Contact the deposit protection scheme your landlord used if you can't get your deposit back.

Houses in Multiple Occupation

Your home is a House in Multiple Occupation (HMO) if both of the following apply:

- at least 3 tenants live there, forming more than 1 household
- you share toilet, bathroom or kitchen facilities with other tenants

Your home is a large HMO if all of the following apply:
- it's at least 3 storeys high
- at least 5 tenants live there, forming more than 1 household
- you share toilet, bathroom or kitchen facilities with other tenants

A household is either a single person or members of the same family who live together. A family includes people who aremarried or living together - including people in same-sex relationships, relatives or half-relatives, eg grandparents, aunts, uncles, siblings, step-parents and step-children.

Standards, obligations and how to complain

If you live in a large HMO, your landlord must meet certain standards and obligations. Contact your local council to report hazards in your HMO. The council is responsible for enforcing HMO standards and can make a landlord take action to correct any problems.

Anti-social behaviour

Report anti-social behaviour to your local council. You council can take over the management of a property to stop anti-social behaviour. It can also create a 'selective licensing scheme' if people in several houses in an area are behaving anti-socially. All landlords of properties in that area must then have a licence to show they're meeting minimum standards.

Complaints

If you have a problem with your landlord: Complain to your landlord - they should have a complaints policy that you can follow, make a complaint to a 'designated person' (your MP, a local councillor or a tenant panel) if you can't resolve the problem with your landlord. contact the Housing Ombudsman if you and your landlord still can't resolve the problem.

Housing Ombudsman

info@housing-ombudsman.org.uk
Telephone: 0300 111 3000

Disabled Facilities Grants

You could get a grant from your council if you're disabled and need to make changes to your home, for example to widen doors and install ramps, improve access to rooms and facilities - eg stairlifts or a downstairs bathroom, provide a heating system suitable for your needs, adapt heating or lighting controls to make them easier to use.

A Disabled Facilities Grant will not affect any benefits that you're getting. How much you get depends on your household income and household savings over £6,000

Country	Grant
England	Up to £30,000
Wales	Up to £36,000
Northern	Up to £25,000

Country	Grant
Ireland	
Scotland	Disabled Facilities Grants are not available - find out about support for equipment and adaptations

Depending on your income, you may need to pay towards the cost of the work to the property. Disabled children under 18 can get a grant without their parents' income being taken into account. Contact your local council for more information. You might not get any grant if you start work on your property before the council approves your application.

How and when you will be paid

You'll be paid either by instalments - as the work progresses or in full - when the work is finished. The council may pay the contractor directly, or give you a cheque to pass on - they'll agree this with you when they approve your application. You'll be paid either when the council is happy with the finished work, when you give the council the invoice, demand or receipt for payment from the contractor. Normally, if you (or a relative) does the work the council will only accept invoices for materials or services you've bought.

Eligibility

You or someone living in your property must be disabled. Either you or the person you're applying for must:

- o own the property or be a tenant
- o intend to live in the property during the grant period (which is currently 5 years)
- o You can also apply for a grant if you're a landlord and have a disabled tenant.

The council will needsto be happy that the work is necessary and appropriate to meet the disabled person's needs, reasonable and can be done - depending on the age and condition of the property. You might not get any grant if you start work on your property before the council approves your application.

Planning and building regulations approval
You need to apply separately for any planning permission or building regulations approval. The council may ask you to employ a qualified architect or surveyor to plan and oversee the work.

How to claim
You'll need to find out:

- what changes are needed to your property
- the type of work that needs to be done
- the cost of the work
- An occupational therapist can look at your circumstances and recommend the type of changes needed.

To get an application form, contact the housing or environment health department of your local council. The council will normally need 2 written estimates for the work. They may be able to give you a list of builders or advise you about employing one.

You can appeal a decision about your Disabled Facilities Grant if you're unhappy with it. Ask your local council for their appeals and complaints procedure. If you appeal and you're still not happy, you can complain to the Local Government Ombudsman.

Other help in the home
There are specialist advice agencies, called Home Improvement Agencies (sometimes called Care and Repair or Staying Put) that will give specialist advice to older and vulnerable householders and

also to people living in private rented accommodation. They are small scale, not-for-profit organisations, usually managed locally by housing associations, councils or charities. They will usually offer practical help with tasks such as arranging a condition survey, getting estimates from builders (trusted builders) applying for grants or loans and also keeping an eye on the progress of work. They may charge a fee towards their assistance, which is usually included in the grant or loans that you may be in receipt of.

To find out whether there is a home improvement agency in your area, you should contact your local council housing department or Foundations (the National Co-ordinating Body for Home Improvement Agencies) address at the rear of the book.

If there is no Home Improvement Agency in your area you might want to engage a surveyor to carry one out for you. As these are costly, or can be, you should always ask what the cost will be first. The Chartered Surveyor Voluntary Service exists to help people who would other wise be able to get professional advice. You need to be referred to them by a Citizens Advice Bureau first.

Disabled people and buying a home

If you want to apply for a mortgage, either to buy a new property or re-mortgage an existing one, it is important to make sure you are well prepared and seek professional advice.

Getting a mortgage if you're in receipt of sickness benefits or disability benefits

If your income is either partially or mainly made up of benefits, this shouldn't stop you from getting a mortgage. Some lenders are more likely than others to accept disability benefits as income when doing their affordability checks.

Benefit related income that may be considered by potential lending partners:

Employment Support Allowance – 100% of this benefit can be used when assessing what a potential home buyer can afford. This can also be done where the applicant has no employment income.

Disability Living Allowance - 100% of this benefit can be used when assessing what a potential home buyer can afford. This can also be done where the applicant has no employment income.

Personal Independent Payment – 100% of this benefit can be used when assessing what a potential homebuyer can afford. This can also be done where the applicant has no employment income.

Carers Allowance – 100%of this benefit can be used when assessing what a potential home buyer can afford. This can also be done where the applicant has no employment income.

Child Benefit - 100% of this benefit can be used when assessing what a potential home buyer can afford. This can also be done where the applicant has no employment income.

Child and Working Tax Credits - 100% of this benefit can be used when assessing what a potential home buyer can afford. This can also be done where the applicant has no employment income.

Part time income - 100%of this benefit can be used when assessing what a potential home buyer can afford. This can also be done where the applicant has no employment income.

Income Support - 100% of this benefit can be used when assessing what a potential home buyer can afford. This can also be done where the applicant has no employed income. To take the benefit into consideration the applicant must be in receipt of either Disability Living Allowance or Personal Independent Payment.

Help with mortgage interest payments

If you're claiming a benefit such as income-related Employment and Support Allowance or Income Support you might be able to claim help with your mortgage interest payments. This is called Support for Mortgage Interest. (SMI). If you qualify for SMI you'll get help paying the interest (but not the capital repayments) on up to £200,000 of your mortgage. You can claim this support even if you are in receipt of benefits when you apply for your mortgage. However, please note that not all lenders will count Support for Mortgage Interest as income when deciding whether or not to lend to you.

The Department for Work and Pensions (DWP) can reduce the amount of support you get if it deems your home is too big or is located in an area that is too expensive. If this happens to you, you should explain to the DWP why you need a larger home (for example, you have a live-in carer or need to keep lots of bulky equipment at home),or need to live in a particular area (for example, you have to be near family or a particular hospital);

SMI will only repay the interest on the loan, it will not repay the capital nor will it repay, for example, the insurance premium element in an endowment mortgage. For this reason the approach most commonly adopted is to raise an interest only mortgage. Find out more about Support for Mortgage Interest on the Gov.uk website

Solicitors

You will have to pay the costs involved such as valuation and legal fees, estate agents fees, advertising, disconnection charges and removal costs.

Adaptations

Some people will require some alteration or adaptation to the property. Read above for information on DFG's.

Before you buy your home and move in, it is important that you make sure the help and support you need is already in place. You can discuss this with Adult Social Care.

Your legal rights

If you can afford a mortgage, banks and other lenders are not allowed to reject your application just because you are disabled. Equally, lenders cannot insist that you pay a larger deposit or make larger monthly repayments than non-disabled customers.

****

Chapter 11

Disabled People and Travel

The Equality Act 2010

As we have seen, the Equality Act 2010 is the main Act covering the rights of disabled people. This is the Act that affects people and Transport.

If you're disabled or have reduced mobility you have certain rights under the Equality Act 2010 and also European Union law when you're travelling by air. If you are travelling outside the European Union, you should find out what help will be available from the airline and the airport where you're travelling.

You don't have to be permanently disabled to get help when you're travelling. For example, you may have reduced mobility because you find it difficult to get about because of your age or a short-term injury or illness.

Bus companies have to make sure that disabled people can get on and off buses in safety and without unreasonable difficulty. They should also make sure that you can travel in safety and reasonable comfort.

Ease of use of public transport

Buses or coaches may need to meet the Public Service Vehicle Accessibility Regulations 2000 allowing access to the vehicle for disabled passengers. In the main, vehicles must meet the regulations if they carry more than 22 passengers and were bought into service from 2000 onwards. Buses and coaches covered by the regulations must have:

o   space for a standard wheelchair

- o a boarding device to enable wheelchair users to get on and off
- o a minimum number of priority seats for disabled passengers
- o handrails to assist disabled people
- o colour contrasting of handrails and steps to help partially sighted people
- o easy to use bell pushes
- o equipment to display the route and destination.

Older buses have to be made accessible to wheelchair users or fitted with accessibility facilities between 2015 and 2020. The speed at which older buses are being replaced by wheelchair user friendly vehicles varies from area to area.

As a wheelchair user you should be able to travel by bus if there is a wheelchair space available and the bus is not full. But you may find you can't if:

- o your chair is very heavy or very big - taking up a space when you are in it of more than 700 mm wide or 1200 mm long
- o you need to travel with your legs fully extended or the backrest reclined.

You must make sure that your wheelchair is in a safe condition to travel. If you have a powered chair you must make sure that the battery is secure. If your chair has adjustable kerb climbers you should check that they are set so that they don't catch on the ramp.

The bus company has the right to refuse to let you travel if they believe that your wheelchair is not in a safe condition.

Wheelchair priority

Wheelchair users should be given priority over pushchair users. If there is a pushchair in the wheelchair space when you try to board the bus the driver should ask the pushchair user to move. However if the pushchair user refuses to move, the driver can't force them to do so.

Boarding or alighting

Buses will have different accessibility features, depending on when they were brought into service. Some buses will be fitted with a portable ramp, steps or vehicle lowering systems. If the bus has these facilities, you must be able to use them unless the conditions of the road make it impossible. If you want the driver or conductor to help you get on or off a bus you should ask for assistance. The driver or conductor should help although they can refuse if they have health and safety concerns.

Complaining about the bus service

If you're dissatisfied with disability access to your bus service or the way you were treated by staff you can make a complaint by following the bus company's complaints procedure.

Rights of disabled passengers using trains

Train operators have to make sure that disabled people have reasonable access to rail travel. Under Rail vehicle accessibility regulations disabled people have rights when travelling by train. Disabled people should be able to get on and off trains in safety and without unreasonable difficulty and do so in a wheelchair and travel in safety and reasonable comfort and do so while in a wheelchair.

All trains which came into service after 31 December 1998 must reach certain standards to meet the accessibility needs of disabled people. For example doorways must be wide enough for wheelchairs, there must be a boarding device (a lift or ramp), all floors must be slip-resistant. All trains will have to meet these accessibility standards by 1 January 2020.

Before you travel

You may need assistance when making a journey by train, i.e. help getting on or off the train, ramps for a wheelchair, a visually-impaired person may need to be guided onto the train.

If you need assistance, you should contact the train company that manages the station you're starting your journey from. You can find out which train company you need to speak to and contact telephone numbers for assisted travel through National Rail Enquiries. Most mainline stations have a member of staff who deals with requests for assistance. That person will be able to make any arrangements you need with other trains companies.

If at all possible, you should give at least 24 hours notice before your journey as this allows time for special arrangements to be made. If this is not possible the train companies will usually always still do their best to help, but provide a guarantee to provide their normal level of service.

On the train

On mainline trains there is a space designed for wheelchair users to travel in safety and comfort. You must always use this space and should apply your brakes when the train is moving. If you use a powered wheelchair, you should make sure that the power is switched off when travelling. All intercity train services and most other mainline services are wheelchair accessible. Access to the train is provided by a ramp kept either at the station or on the train.

Wheelchair accessible sleeper cabins are available on overnight trains between London and Scotland but not on those between London and the West of England.

Most local and regional train trains can accommodate wheelchair users. New trains also have facilities to assist sensory impaired people - for example, public information systems that are both visual and audible. An increasing number of trains have wheelchair accessible toilets. You can find out about the facilities on any train when booking your ticket.

It is important to note that train staff have a legal duty to make reasonable adjustments to accommodate disabled passengers, for example, allowing you to travel in first class on a standard class ticket if the accessible toilet in standard class is out of order.

Some train companies have trains that cannot accommodate mobility scooters. Contact the train company before travelling to check they can safely accommodate your scooter.

Complaining about a train company

If you're dissatisfied with disability access on your train service or the way you were treated by staff you can make a complaint. You should try and check the station or train operator's disabled people's protection policy. This will be available from the company's customer services officer or on their website. If the train company hasn't followed the policy, you can complain, using the train company's complaints procedure.

Find out contact telephone numbers for assisted travel through National Rail Enquiries Tel – 0845 748 4950. If you aren't happy with the way a train company deals with your complaint you can appeal, outside London, to: Passenger Focus (tel: 0300 123 2350).

In London-London Travel Watch at:
http://www.londontravelwatch.org.uk/ (tel: 020 3176 2999).

Disabled people and air travel

As with other modes of transport, UK airports are covered by the rules in the Equality Act 2010. They must provide facilities and information that can be used by everyone whatever your needs. For example, if you're in a wheelchair or you're visually impaired, you should be able to read departure boards easily or be able to access all areas of the airport.

Reserving seats

If you book your tickets on-line, there should be sections on the on-line form you can fill in to give the airline notice of the help you are likely to need. If you book your tickets over the phone, or face-to-face, you should be given as much information as possible to make sure you can make a booking that's suitable for your needs.

Get any confirmation that you need assistance in writing. This means you will have proof that you made a special request if the help you need isn't available when you fly and you need to take this further. You should be allowed to book seats which meet your particular needs. If the airline doesn't pre-book seats you should be allowed to board the plane before other passengers.

At the airport

You should contact customer services at the airport if you need help to move through the airport from check-in, through security to the departure gate. For staff to help you, you must give at least 48 hours notice before you are due to fly, turn up at the agreed time, and give yourself enough time to move through the airport. As with all passengers, it is recommended that you turn up at least two hours before departure. If your flight is changed, the airport should still make reasonable efforts to try and help you.

However, the airline should also tell you that it may not be possible to guarantee your seat if there is problem. For example, it may be that someone with a greater need than you needs the seat, or there's a change of plane with different seating arrangements. If your seat does have to be changed, staff should still make every effort to find a way to accommodate you.

The airline will usually have its own policy about how it can help you if you need extra seats because of your disability and the number of bookings it will accept may be limited, depending on when and where you fly.

Moving around the airport

The airport has a legal duty to help you with the following things when you arrive:

- make sure airport staff know you have arrived and if necessary meet you at an agreed meeting point. This could be either inside or outside the terminal
- help you move from the meeting point to check-in
- help you check in your baggage
- help you get from check-in to the plane, taking you through passport control, customs and security checks
- board the plane with assisted help if you need it
- settle into your seat
- help with your cabin baggage
- help to get from your seat to the aircraft door
- help you get off the aircraft, with assisted help if you need it
- help you get to baggage reclaim and go through passport control, customs and security
- help you get to a point where you can carry on with your journey
- help with connecting flights
- help you to reach a toilet.

Complaining

If you have a problem with the help you've got from an airline or airport because of your disability or reduced mobility you may want to complain. It is recommended that you should first do this directly with them and try and sort out the problem. If you can't manage to sort out the problem, you can complain to the Civil Aviation Authority (CAA) at the address below:

Passenger Advice and Complaints Team
4th Floor,

CAA House
45-59 Kingsway
London
WC2B 6TE

Rights on the plane

You should always let your airline know of any special needs at least 48 hours before you fly. However even if you don't give 48 hours notice, the airline should still make reasonable efforts to help you.

An airline can't refuse to let you to board the plane because you're disabled or have reduced mobility. However, they can refuse to let you to fly if:

- o you haven't told your booking agent, tour operator or airline that you have a disability or reduced mobility at least 48 hours before you fly
- o there are safety reasons which prevent you from flying - for example you're flying alone but you need help to get about safely
- o the aircraft doors are too small.

If there's a safety reason that you can't fly or the aircraft doors are too small, the airline should try to find another way of getting to you to your destination. If this isn't possible, you should be entitled to a refund.

On the plane

If you're likely to need help to do certain things on the plane, for example fastening your seatbelt, going to the toilet or getting to an emergency exit, the airline can insist that you travel with someone you know. Airline staff don't have to give you personal care.

Taking equipment on a plane

You should be allowed to take up to two mobility items on board with you that will help you get around. If you need more equipment that needs to be checked in, ask if the airline is willing to carry it.

Disabled people and Taxi travel

Taxi drivers and companies have to make sure that disabled people can get in and out of taxis and minicabs in safety and without unreasonable difficulty. They should also make sure that you can travel in safety and reasonable comfort. It is important to note that licensed taxis are only required to be wheelchair accessible in some cities. To find out if there are accessible taxis near you, contact the taxi licensing office at your local council. Another important point is that all taxis and minicabs have a duty to carry assistance dogs.

Ease of use

Their are no national standards for wheelchair accessible taxis and minicabs. Local authorities are in charge of accessibility policies. In London all taxis must be able to carry a standard wheelchair. To find out more about the situation in your area you should contact your local authority.

All drivers must make reasonable adjustments by changing practices, policies and procedures which put disabled people at a serious disadvantage when trying to use their services. Making reasonable adjustments includes: the driver guiding or helping you into the vehicle; helping you to get out of the vehicle at your destination and the taxi or mincicab firm having a standard training programme to include disability awareness for all drivers.

Drivers of licensed taxis and minicabs must allow you to travel with a guide dog, a hearing dog or any other assistance dog free of charge. A driver can be prosecuted for refusing to let you take an assistance dog or charging extra to carry it. However, a driver may be able to get an exemption certificate. This allows them to refuse to take an assistance dog for medical reasons. If they have an exemption certificate, it must be displayed in the vehicle.

Complaining about taxis and minicabs

You should make your complaint to your local council who deal with taxi licensing. In London, you should complain to the Public Carriage Office (PCO). You can complain by telephone, letter or email. Website www.pco-licence.co.uk.

To complain about a minicab, also known as private hire vehicles, you should first try and sort out the problem with the minicab firm. If you aren't happy with the outcome or feel your complaint is more serious, you can complain to your local council, most have taxi complaint forms on their websites, in London complain to the PCO.

When you make a complaint about a taxi or minicab, it's helpful to have the vehicle registration number of the taxi or minicab. This will be printed on the number plate or disc, the taxi or minicab licence number, the taxi driver's badge number – which you can normally get from their badge - or the name of the minicab firm.

Disabled people and cruise ships

Cruise ships, as with all modes of transport are affected by the Equality Act 2010. Many cruise ships are now fully accessible to people with a wide range of disabilities providing some of the most exciting, inspiring and best value-for-money holidays that you can find. Newer ships offer purpose built accessible cabins, entertainment venues and facilities, wide gangways and lifts whilst moving round the ship, and accessible embarkation and disembarkation. Many older ships have been adapted to accommodate disabled cruisers, meaning that disability is no longer a prohibitive factor in going on a cruise.

For more information on disabiled access and holidays on cruise ships go to: www.disabledholidaydirectory.co.uk

The Blue Badge Scheme
The Blue Badge scheme provides a range of parking benefits for disabled people with severe walking difficulties who travel either as drivers or as passengers.

Vehicle tax exemption-Eligibility
You can apply for exemption from paying vehicle tax if you get the:
- o higher rate mobility component of Disability Living Allowance (DLA)
- o enhanced rate mobility component of Personal Independence Payment (PIP)

War Pensioner's Mobility Supplement
The vehicle must be registered in the disabled person's name or their nominated driver's name. It must only be used for the disabled person's personal needs. It can't be used by the nominated driver for their own personal use.

How to claim
You claim the exemption when you apply for vehicle tax. You can do this online, by phone, by post or at a Post Office that deals with vehicle tax. You'll need:
- o your exemption certificate serial number
- o the surname, date of birth and National Insurance number of the exemption certificate holder
- o Your exemption certificate must be one of the following:
- o certificate of entitlement for DLA
- o statement of entitlement for PIP
- o annual certificate of entitlement

You must claim at a Post Office that deals with vehicle tax if you're claiming for a particular vehicle for the first time. You can't do it online or by phone.

Vehicle tax reduction-Eligibility

You can get a 50% reduction in vehicle tax if you get the PIP standard rate mobility component. You can't get a reduction for getting the DLA lower rate mobility component.

How to claim

Send all of the following to DVLA Swansea:

- o your statement of entitlement (it's at the end of your PIP award letter)
- o the vehicle registration certificate (V5C)
- o a V10 form
- o an original MOT or GVT certificate (if your vehicle needs one)
- o a cheque or payable order (made out to 'DVLA, Swansea') for 50% of the full rate of car tax for the vehicle

DVLA
Swansea
SA99 1DZ

The Motability Scheme

The Motability Scheme can help you with leasing a car, powered wheelchair or scooter. You'll need to be getting one of the following:

- o the higher rate of the mobility component of DLA
- o War Pensioners' Mobility Supplement
- o the enhanced rate of the mobility component of PIP

o VAT relief for vehicles

You may not have to pay VAT on having a vehicle adapted to suit your condition, or on the lease of a Motability vehicle - this is known as VAT relief.

Community and public transport

Your local council may operate dial-a-ride or taxi schemes, for example, using vouchers or tokens. You may also be eligible for a bus pass and/or Disabled Persons Railcard.

Specialist holiday companies

There are numerous specialist holiday companies and also organisations offering holidays and breaks for disabled people-see useful addresses and websites at the back of the book for further information.

****

Ch.12

Disability and the Armed Forces

War Disablement Pension

You can claim a War Disablement Pension if you are no longer Serving in HM Armed Forces and you have a disablement (i.e. an injury, illness or disease) that you consider was caused or made worse by service before 6 April 2005. If you think your disablement was caused by service on or after 6 April 2005, you should claim under the Armed Forces Compensation Scheme. Claims can be made for both physical and mental conditions.

There are no time limits for claiming under the War Pension Scheme but claims can only be considered once your service has ended and payment will usually be made from the date of claim

Armed Forces Compensation Scheme (AFCS)

AFCS provides compensation for any injury, illness or death which is caused by service on or after 6 April 2005. The War Pension Scheme (WPS) compensates for any injury, illness or death which occurs up to this date. The AFCS is a no-fault Scheme which means payment is made without admitting fault. It is entirely separate from any other personal accident cover, such as PAX or SLI. Therefore, any accident cover that you may already hold is not taken into account when determining an AFCS award.

All current and former members of the UK Armed Forces, including Reservists, may submit a claim for compensation. Unlike the War Pension Scheme, you can submit an AFCS claim while still serving, as well as after you have left the Armed Forces. While there are time limits, above all you should submit a claim for compensation at a time which is best for you. In the event of service-related death, the Scheme pays benefits to eligible partners and children. An 'eligible partner' is someone with whom you are cohabiting in an exclusive and substantial relationship, with financial and wider dependence.

The Service Personnel and Veterans Agency (SPVA)

This agency is part of the Ministry of Defence and provides a range of 'through life' support function to around 900,000 serving ex-Service personnel. These include the delivery of HR, pay and pension schemes to the Armed Forces, compensation payments for those injured or bereaved though Service, provision of MOD medals and one to one help and support for veterans.

Service Personnel and Veterans Agency

Tomlinson House, Norcross
Thornton-Cleveleys
FY5 3WP
Telephone:Veterans-UK: Helpline 0800 169 22 77
Minicom (textphones) 0800 169 3458
O/seas: +44 1253 866043

Email: Veterans.help@spva.gsi.gov.uk
Website: http://www.veterans-uk.info

Veterans UK

www.veterans-uk.info
Veterans-UK is the name used for the veterans advice services provided by the Service Personnel and Veterans Agency. It's the first stop for veterans who need help and support. A veteran is anyone who has served in HM Armed Forces, regular or reserve including National Servicemen. Veteran's status also applies to former Polish forces under British command in WWII and Merchant Mariners who have seen duty in military operations. Veterans can be any age

from 18 to 100 plus. Veterans need not have served overseas or in conflict.

Veterans Welfare Service

The Veterans Welfare Service (VWS) is committed to enhancing the quality of life for Veterans and beneficiaries of SPVA pensions and compensation schemes, and all their dependants. It also focuses upon providing support that will enable the seamless transition from Service to Civilian life, assist bereaved families or respond to key life events that present welfare needs. It achieves this by adopting a single central coordinating role that facilitates access to all appropriate services.

The VWS provides a caseworker approach that offers professional help and guidance through either telephone contact or a dedicated visiting service, Under Veterans UK the VWS works in collaborative partnerships with the tri-Services, ex-Service charities, statutory and non-statutory bodies, local community service providers and Veterans Advisory & Pensions Committee's to deliver a quality welfare service that promotes independence, maintains dignity and provides continuous support through life.

The SPVA Veterans Welfare Service has five Welfare Centres, providing advice and support across the UK.

The contact details for each office are:

Norcross (based near Blackpool)
Tel 01253 333494
Email SPVA-VWSNorcross@mod.uk

Kidderminster (based in Worcester)
Tel 01562 825527
Email SPVA-VWSKidderminster@mod.uk

Centurion (based in Gosport)
Tel 02392 702232
Email SPVAVWSCENTURION@SPVA.mod.uk

Imjin (based in Gloucester)
Tel 01452 510825
Email VWS-innsworth@spva.mod.uk

NHS treatment

If you need an examination or treatment relating to the condition for which you receive a war pension, you are entitled to be given priority for NHS services, subject only to the needs of emergency and other urgent cases.

If you experience difficulty arranging treatment, tell the War Pensions treatment Section. In certain circumstances, your doctor may be able to arrange for you to be admitted to a Ministry of Defence services hospital for the treatment of the disability for which you receive your war pension. If so, you will be eligible for help with travelling costs.

Equipment for mobility

If you need equipment as a result of the disability for which you receive a war pension, you will be able to get advice from the The SPVA Veterans Welfare Service . Equipment such as wheelchairs, artificial limbs, or home nursing equipment can be obtained from the NHS. The organisations and charities below may also be able to assist in providing or funding equipment for your special needs.

The Royal British Legion is the nation's leading Armed Forces charity providing care and support to all members of the Armed Forces past and present and their families. They can provide advice on disability claims, loans for home improvements, run residential care homes, offer holiday breaks for carers and much more.

Tel: 0808 802 8080 Website: http://www.britishlegion.org.uk.

Royal British Legion Scotland
Benevolence and Comradeship.
Logie Green Road
Edinburgh
EH7 4HR
Tel:: 0131 557 2782
Fax:: 0131 557 5819
Website: http://www.rblscotland.com

BLESMA (British Limbless Ex-Servicemen's Association) assists men and women who have lost their limbs through service in the armed forces or as a result of it. BLESMA provides permanent residential accommodation, gives advice on pensions and allowances, provides financial assistance to members and widows, runs a welfare visiting service, plans and organises rehabilitation programmes for amputees an helps in finding suitable employment. Tel: 0208 590 1124 Website: http://www.blesma.org

The **Burma Star Association** provides a welfare service and gives free and confidential advice to all holders of the Burma Star. Tel: 0207 823 4273.
Website:http://www.burmastar.org.uk

Combat Stress is the UK's leading military charity specialising in the care of Veterans' mental health. They look after men and women who are suffering from a psychological condition related to their Service career. This might be depression, anxiety, a phobia or PTSD (Post Traumatic Stress Disorder). Their services are free of charge to the Veteran.
Website: http://www.combatstress.com

The "Not Forgotten" Association provides holidays, television sets, licences, outings, excursions and entertainment for disabled ex-service people. Tel: 020 7730 2400
Website:http://www.nfassociation.org/

The Royal Air Forces Association gives advice and financial assistance to serving or ex-serving RAF personnel and their dependents through a network of branches. Each branch has an honorary welfare officer who will assess requests for help and complete the appropriate forms for assistance. The Association also runs a nursing home and three convalescent home together with supportive and sheltered housing schemes.
Tel: 020 8994 8504. Website: http://www.rafa.org.uk

The Royal Alfred Seafarer's Society provides accommodation for ex-members of the Royal Navy and Merchant Navy at three separate establishments in Surrey and Sussex, offering, respectively, sheltered housing, residential and nursing care.
Tel: 020 8401 2889 Website: http://www.royalalfredseafarers.co.uk/

Blind Veterans UK (St Dunstan's sicnce 1915): - Established in 1915, St Dunstan's provide essential training and rehabilitation for ex-Service men and women who are now blinded due to war, age, accident or illness.
T: 020 7723 5021
F: 020 7262 6199
Website: www.blindveterans.org.uk/

The Soldiers, Sailors, Airmen and Families Association (SSAFA Forces Help) offers welfare help, advice and support to serving and ex-serving members of the armed forces, including partners, widows/widowers and dependent children. They also help obtain equipment and aids and provide specially designed permanent and holiday accommodation for disabled people, and residential care homes. Local branches nationwide and in Eire can raise grant aid through service charities and other sources. Contact local Branch (see local phone book) or the Welfare Department at Central Office.

Tel: 020 7403 8783. Website:http://www.ssafa.org.uk

****

Chapter 13

Income Tax and Disabled People

For income tax purposes, the situation for disabled people is the same as for anyone else, with a few exceptions.

Tax basics

Each person in the UK is taxed as an individual. Tax is based on income for a tax year. Whilst some types of income is tax free, other income is potentially taxable. Income that is taxable includes earnings from a job you may have, any profits from self employment or business, state and private pensions, some benefits and any other income such as rents receivable, savings interest, dividends from shares etc. Tax relief can be obtained on certain types of spending which is given in two ways:

- By deducting the expense from your total income, thus reducing the amount of income left to be taxed. This applies to contributions to occupational pension schemes and donations to charity through payroll giving
- Through tax relief at source. You deduct tax relief from the payment you are making and handover the remaining reduced amount. If you are a higher rate taxpayer, you can claim extra relief. This method applies to contributions to personal pensions and chartable donations to gift aid.

Personal allowances

Every individual has a personal allowance. There are annually published individual allowances, which may vary according to individual circumstances. The tables below shows the annual allowances applicable for 2015/16. They also indicate previous years allowances. The allowances are higher for people aged between 65-74 and higher again for people over 75. However, you will lose this extra age-related allowance if your income exceeds the threshold shown below. The extra allowance is reduced by £1 for every £2 by which your income exceeds the threshold.

Personal Allowances

The Personal Allowance is the amount of income a person can get before they pay tax.

Allowances	2015 to 2016	2014 to 2015	2013 to 2014	2012 to 2013
Personal Allowance for people born after 5 April 1948	£10,600	£10,000	£9,440	£8,105
Income limit for Personal Allowance	£100,000	£100,000	£100,000	£100,000

Personal Allowances for people born before 6 April 1948

People born before 6 April 1948 may be entitled to a bigger personal Allowance. From 2015 to 2016, people born after 5 April 1938 get the standard Personal Allowance.

Allowances	2015 to 2016	2014 to 2015	2013 to 2014
Personal Allowance for people born between 6 April 1938 and 5 April 1948	£10,600	£10,500	£10,500
Personal Allowance for people born before 6 April 1938	£10,660	£10,660	£10,660
Income limit for Personal Allowance	£27,700	£27,000	£26,100

This Personal Allowance goes down by £1 for every £2 above the income limit. It won't go below the standard Personal Allowance for that year. There's more guidance about Personal Allowances for people born before 6 April 1948.

Before 2013 to 2014

Before the 2013 to 2014 tax year, the bigger Personal Allowance was based on age instead of date of birth.

Allowances	2012 to 2013
Personal Allowance for people aged 65 to 74	£10,500
Personal Allowance for people aged 75 and over	£10,660
Income limit for Personal Allowance	£25,400

Other allowances

Allowances	2015 to 2016	2014 to 2015	2013 to 2014	2012 to 2013
Married Couple's Allowance - maximum amount	£8,355	£8,165	£7,915	£7,705
Married Couple's Allowance - minimum amount	£3,220	£3,140	£3,040	£2,960
Blind Person's Allowance	£2,290	£2,230	£2,160	£2,100

Tax rates and bands

Tax is paid on the amount of taxable income remaining after allowances have been deducted.

Band	Rate	Income after allowances 2015 to 2016	Income after allowances 2014 to 2015	Income after allowances 2013 to 2014	Income after allowances 2012 to 2013
Starting rate	10% (0%	Up to £5,000	Up to £2,880	Up to £2,790	Up to £2,710

Band	Rate	Income after allowances 2015 to 2016	Income after allowances 2014 to 2015	Income after allowances 2013 to 2014	Income after allowances 2012 to 2013
for savings	from 2015 to 2016)				
Basic rate	20%	Up to £31,785	Up to £31,865	Up to £32,010	Up to £34,370
Higher rate	40%	£31,786 to £150,000	£31,866 to £150,000	£32,011 to £150,000	£34,371 to £150,000
Additional rate	45%	Over £150,001	Over £150,001	Over £150,001	N/A
Additional rate	50%	N/A	N/A	N/A	Over £150,001

Dividends

The following rates for tax on dividends apply from 6 April 2010 to the present tax year.

Band	Dividend tax rates	Rate adjusted for dividend tax credit
Basic rate (and non-taxpayers)	10%	0%
Higher rate	32.5%	25%
Additional rate (from 6 April 2013)	37.5%	30.56%
Additional rate (dividends paid before 6 April 2013)	42.5%	36.11%

Allowances for blind people

A blind person's allowance is available if you are registered blind in England or would be unable to carry out any work for which normal eyesight is needed (Scotland and Northern Ireland). In either case, this means that you have been certified as blind or severely sight impaired by a consultant opthalmologist. The allowance is £2,290 in 2015/16.

If your income is too low for you to be able to use all or part of your blind person's allowance, you can request your tax office to transfer the surplus to your spouse or civil partner to reduce their tax burden.

The Married Couple's allowance

This particular allowance is restricted to married couples and civil partners where one or both of the couple were born before 6th April 1935. In 2015/16 the allowance is £8,355, with a minimum amount of £3,220. Married couples allowance works differently to other allowances in that you get a reduction in your tax bill equal to 10% of the allowance or the amount needed to reduce your tax bill to zero (whichever is lower). Married couples allowance is initially given to the husband (if you were married before 5th December 2005 or whoever has the higher income where your marriage or civil partnership took place on or after that date). If the person who has the allowance has income above the age related allowance threshold (£27,700 in 2015/16) the married couple's allowance is reduced by £1 for every £2 of income over the threshold. However, married couples allowance is never reduced below a basic amount (£3,220 in 2015/16). Age related personal allowance is reduced before any married couples allowance. Whoever initially gets the married couples allowance, part or all of the basic amount can be transferred to the other spouse or partner.

Tax-free income

These are the main types of income likely to be relevant that are free from income tax.

o   Pensions and state benefits

o   £10 Christmas bonus for state pensioners and also the one-off £60 Christmas bonus introduced in 2009

- o Winter fuel payment
- o Pension credit
- o Working tax credit
- o Housing benefit (note changes to benefits with introduction of Universal credits in October 2013)
- o Bereavement payment (lump sum for widows and widowers)
- o Council tax benefit (as above changes withy the introduction of universal credit)
- o Disability living allowance and attendance allowance (Renamed Personal Independent Payments from 2013)
- o Any additional occupational pensions arising as a result of injury at work
- o Tax free lump sum from a pension scheme

Income from an employer

- o Some fringe benefits, such as employers pensions contributions
- o Mileage allowance
- o Up to £30,000 redundancy payment
- o Up to £3 a week to cover the extra cost of working from home
- o Long service award that is not cash and has been given for £20 or more years service

Benefits that are taxable

The following benefits are taxable:

- o Bereavement allowance, widowed mothers/parent's allowance and widows pension
- o Carer's allowance
- o Contributory employment and support allowance

- o Long term incapacity benefit (but not if you transferred from invalidity benefit)
- o Income support (if you are directly involved in a trade dispute)
- o Invalidity allowance (paid with a state pension)
- o Industrial death benefit
- o Job seekers allowance
- o State pension
- o Statutory adoption pay, statutory maternity pay
- o Statutory paternity pay and statutory sick pay

****

Chapter 14

Useful Contacts

The Law and Disability

Disability Law Service
The Foundry
17 Oval Way
London
SE11 5RR
www.advice.dis.org.yk
advice@dis.org.yk
Free legal advice 0207 7919 800

Gov.uk
www.gov.uk/rights-disabled-person/overview

The Benefit System

Attendance Allowance helpline 0845 605 6055 or 0345 605 6055
(textphone: 0845 604 5312)

Carer's Allowance Unit 0845 608 4321 (textphone: 0845 604
5312)

DWP Bereavement Service:

Telephone: 0845 606 0265
Textphone: 0845 606 0285

Telephone: 0845 606 0275 (Welsh)
Textphone: 0845 606 0295 (Welsh)

Department for Work and Pensions (DWP) on 0800 917 2222 (textphone 0800 917 777).

Disability benefits Advice
www.gov.uk/disability-benefits-helpline

Jobcentre Plus 0800 055 6688 textphone 0800 023 4888

Pension Credit claim line 0800 99 1234 (textphone: 0800 169 0133).

Royal National Institute for the Blind 0303 123 9999 www.rnib.org.uk.

Tax Credit helpline 0345 300 3900 (textphone 0345 300 3909).

TV Licence concessions 0300 790 6165

Universal Credit helpline 0845 600 0723 (textphone 0845 600 0743).

Victim Support line 0845 30 30 900 (England and Wales) or 0845 60 39 213 (Scotland)

website www.victimsupportsco.org.uk;
emailsupportline@victimsupport.org.uk
info@victimsupportsco.org.uk

Winter Fuel Payments Helpline 0845 915 1515

Carers and Help For Carers

Carers Trust
Tel: 0844 800 OEH
www.carers.org/getting-help/help-carers

Help and Advice on caring-Carers UK
www.carersuk.org/help-and-advice
Tel; 0808 808 7777

Helping hands Home Care Specialists
www.helpinghandshomecare.co.uk
0843 634 7312

Carers Direct NHS Choices
www.nhs.uk/carersdirect

Carers and help for carers Scotland
0300 123 2008

Wales
0292 009 0087

Disabled People and Employment

Access to Work 020 8426 3110.

www.evenbreak.co.uk Jobs for disabled people - Evenbreak matches disabled job seekers with employers looking to build a diverse workforce

www.gov.uk/rights-disabled-person/employment

Industrial Injuries-Barnsley Industrial Injuries Disablement Benefit centre Telephone: 0345 758 5433

National Careers Service Helpline 0800 100 900 or Skills Development Scotland 0800 917 8000.

Disabled people and Education

Contact a Family helpline

helpline@cafamily.org.uk
Telephone: 0808 808 3555

Independent Parental Special Education Advice (IPSEA).

IPSEA advice line
Telephone: 0800 018 4016

Student finance England 0845 300 5090 www.gov.uk/student-finance

Northern Ireland Student finance NI 0845 600 0662
www.studentfinanceni.co.uk

Scotland Student Awards Agency for Scotland 0300 555 0505
www.saas.gov.uk

Wales Student Finance Wales 0845 602 8845
www.studentfianncewales.co.uk

Care Homes

Care Homes-Support and Guidance NHS Choices
www.nhs.uk/.../Pages/care-homes.aspx
Care Homes for Disabled People

www.newsnow.co.uk/.../care-homes-for-disabled-people

Whilst You Are in Hospital

Disabled People Rights in Hospital
www.nhs.uk/.../Pages/disabled-people-in-hospital.aspx

Tenancy Rights and Rights in the Home

Housing Ombudsman
info@housing-ombudsman.org.uk
Telephone: 0300 111 3000

Shelter England
www.shelter.org.uk
Help line 0808 800 444

Disability Housing Scotland
www.housingoptionsscotland.org.uk

Independent Living For Disabled people
www.scope.org.uk
0808 800 3333
Deals with UK housing advice for disabled

Disabled Children

Child benefit helpline 0300 200 3100: textphone 0300 200 3103

Council for Disabled Children
www.councilfordisabledchildren.org.uk Tel: 0207 843 1900

Every Disabled Child Matters
www.edcm.org.uk
Tel: 0207843 6082

Family Fund 0844 974 4099 Online www.familyfund.org.uk

Healthy Start Helpline 0845 607 6823 www.healthystart.nhs.uk

www.nurserymilk.co.uk.

Help if you have a disabled child
www.gov.uk/help-for-disabled-child

KIDS is a leading disabled children's charity that has been in existence for over 40 years working to enable disabled children and young people and their families www.kids.org.uk

Royal National Institute for the Blind 0303 123 9999 www.rnib.org.uk.

Support for Disabled Children
www.actionforchildren.org.uk/what-we-do/support

Vaccine Damage Payments Unit Tel: 01772 899 944 www.gov.uk/vaccine-damage-payment.

_____

Disabled People and Travel
Trains
Complaints and information-National Rail Enquiries Tel – 0845 748 4950. If you aren't happy with the way a train company deals with your complaint you can appeal, outside London, to: Passenger Focus (tel: 0300 123 2350).

In London-London Travel Watch at:
http://www.londontravelwatch.org.uk/ (tel: 020 3176 2999).

Air Travel
Complaints and information- Civil Aviation Authority (CAA) at the address below:

Passenger Advice and Complaints Team
4th Floor,
CAA House
45-59 Kingsway
London
WC2B 6TE

Taxi and Mini cabs
Public Carriage Office (PCO) www.pco-licence.co.uk

Motability
www.motability.co.uk

Blue badge Scheme
www.gov.uk/blue-badge-scheme-information-council

Specialist companies
Access Travel
www.access-travel.co.uk
Te: 01942 888844

Responsible Travel
www.responsibletravel.com Tel: 01273 823 700

Enable Holidays
0871 299 4939

Disability Travel
www.disabilitytravel.com

Disability and the Armed Forces

BLESMA (British Limbless Ex-Servicemen's Association) Tel: 0208 590 1124 Website: http://www.blesma.org

Blind Veterans UK (St Dunstan's sicnce 1915 020 7723 5021 F: 020 7262 6199-Website: www.blindveterans.org.uk/

Burma Star Association Tel: 0207 823 4273.
Website:http://www.burmastar.org.uk

Combat Stress http://www.combatstress.com

Not Forgotten" Association 020 7730 2400
Website:http://www.nfassociation.org/

Royal Air Forces Association Tel: 020 8994 8504. Website: http://www.rafa.org.uk

Royal Alfred Seafarer's Society Tel: 020 8401 2889 Website: http://www.royalalfredseafarers.co.uk/

Royal British Legion
Tel: 0808 802 8080 Website: http://www.britishlegion.org.uk.
Royal British Legion Scotland
Tel:: 0131 557 2782
Fax:: 0131 557 5819
Website: http://www.rblscotland.com

Service Personnel and Veterans Agency
Telephone:Veterans-UK: Helpline 0800 169 22 77
Minicom (textphones) 0800 169 3458
O/seas: +44 1253 866043

Email: Veterans.help@spva.gsi.gov.uk
Website: http://www.veterans-uk.info

Soldiers, Sailors, Airmen and Families Association (SSAFA Forces Help) 020 7403 8783. Website:http://www.ssafa.org.uk

Veterans UK
www.veterans-uk.info

Veterans Welfare Service
Norcross (based near Blackpool)
Tel 01253 333494
Email SPVA-VWSNorcross@mod.uk

Kidderminster (based in Worcester)
Tel 01562 825527
Email SPVA-VWSKidderminster@mod.uk

Centurion (based in Gosport)
Tel 02392 702232
Email SPVAVWSCENTURION@SPVA.mod.uk

Imjin (based in Gloucester)
Tel 01452 510825
Email VWS-innsworth@spva.mod.uk

Income Tax
HMRC Helpline-0843 805 0053

Immigration advice

Immigration Advisory Service
0121 314 9252

Citizens Advice
www.citizensadvice.org.uk/law-and-rights/immigration

Immigration Advice Centre Limited
Specialists in Immigration and Asylum law
01642 219 222

_____

Pensions Advice

The Pensions Advisory Service
www.pensionsadvisoryservice.org.uk
Tel: 0300 123 1047

****

Index

****

www.straightforwardco.co.uk

All titles, listed below, in the Straightforward Guides Series can be purchased online, using credit card or other forms of payment by going to www.straightfowardco.co.uk A discount of 25% per title is offered with online purchases.

Law

A Straightforward Guide to:
Consumer Rights
Bankruptcy Insolvency and the Law
Employment Law
Private Tenants Rights
Family law
Small Claims in the County Court
Contract law
Intellectual Property and the law
Divorce and the law
Leaseholders Rights
The Process of Conveyancing
Knowing Your Rights and Using the Courts
Producing Your own Will
Housing Rights
The Bailiff the law and You
Probate and The Law
Company law
What to Expect When You Go to Court
Guide to Competition Law
Give me Your Money-Guide to Effective Debt Collection
Caring for a Disabled Child

General titles

Letting Property for Profit

Buying, Selling and Renting property

Buying a Home in England and France

Bookkeeping and Accounts for Small Business

Creative Writing

Freelance Writing

Writing Your own Life Story

Writing performance Poetry

Writing Romantic Fiction

Speech Writing

Teaching Your Child to Read and write

Teaching Your Child to Swim

Raising a Child-The Early Years

Creating a Successful Commercial Website

The Straightforward Business Plan

The Straightforward C.V.

Successful Public Speaking

Handling Bereavement

Play the Game-A Compendium of Rules

Individual and Personal Finance

Understanding Mental Illness

Buying and Selling Online

Creating a Successful Franchise

Go to:

www.straightforwardco.co.uk

Titles in the Emerald Explaining Series:

Finding Aspergers in the family

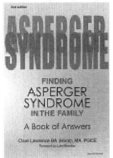

This best selling book in the Emerald Series, *Finding Asperger Syndrome in the Family-A Book of Answers*, 2nd Edition by Clare Lawrence, is a very comprehensive and clear guide to Aspergers Syndrome and the effects on children and family. ISBN 9781847163295 £9.99

Explaining Alzheimers and Dementia

What exactly is Alzheimer's disease and dementia? With Alzheimer's and dementia now reckoned to affect many in our population, this is a question that more and more people are needing to ask. Explaining Alzheimer's and Dementia provides a clear and concise introduction to this fascinating and complex subject. ISBN 9781847161703-£9.99

Explaining Bi-Polar Disorder

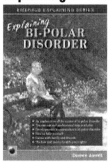

Bi-polar disorder is the term used to describe what was once known as manic depressive illness. Bi-polar disorder is becoming more and more common, particularly in young adults, although people of all age ranges will suffer from the condition. This book, as with all the guides in the *Explaining* series aims to provide an insight into bi-polar disorder and explores the background to the condition, the symptoms and the various treatments on offer. 9781847164131-£9.99

Explaining Parkinson's

Parkinson's, or the onset of Parkinson's, is a very stressful time for those unfortunate to suffer it. Quite often guidance on the subject is conflicting and unclear. Explaining Parkinson's deals with Parkinson's in a very sensitive and clear way and will be of great assistance and comfort to those who read it. The book gives advice on techniques for coping with the diagnosis, finding the right doctors, diets and, overall, dealing with the condition and the attendant stress. ISBN 9781847164230-£9.99

Explaining Depression

Anyone of any age can suffer with depression. One in five adults will suffer with depression in their lifetime, every year, doctors diagnose two million new cases in the UK alone. However, depression can be treated effectively. This concise books offers meaningful insights into the condition and how to combat it.

ISBN 9781847160476- £9.99

Waiting for a Voice

Waiting for a Voice - A Parent's Guide to Coping with Verbal Dyspraxia deals with a condition which is recognized as being quite widespread. Verbal Dyspraxia is a specific, severe speech disorder found in children which prevents the brain from getting the correct messages to the muscles in and around the mouth, which in turn affects the ability to make intelligible speech. ISBN 9781847164827-£9.99

Autism Spectrum Disorder

What is an Autism Spectrum Disorder? With Autism and Asperger syndrome now reckoned to affect one in a hundred of our population, this is a question that more and more people are needing to ask. Explaining Autism and Asperger Syndrome provides a clear and concise introduction to this fascinating and perplexing subject. Written in accessible, non-specialist language it provides an ideal introduction for parents, carers, teachers and employers – for anyone coming across this intriguing condition – on ways to understand what is the Autistic Spectrum.

ISBN 978184761642
£9.99

****